Other titles in the School of Psychotherapy and Counselling (SPC) Series of Regent's College:

Philosophy for Counsellors   Tim Le Bon
Heart of Listening   Rosalind Pearmain

SPC SERIES

Embodied Theories

Edited by

Ernesto Spinelli

and

Sue Marshall

CONTINUUM
London and New York

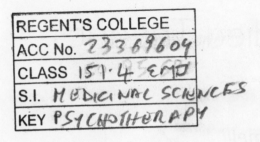

Continuum

The Tower Building
11 York Road
London SE1 7NX

370 Lexington Avenue
New York
NY 10017–6503

www.continuumbooks.com

© 2001 Ernesto Spinelli and Sue Marshall and contributors

First published 2001

British Library Cataloguing-in-Publication Data
A catalogue record for this book is available from the British Library.

ISBN 0–8264–5781–9 (hardback)
ISBN 0–8264–5208–6 (paperback)

Designed and typeset by Kenneth Burnley, Wirral, Cheshire.
Printed and bound in Great Britain by Biddles Ltd, *www.biddles.co.uk*

Contents

Series Editor's Introduction

IT IS BOTH A GREAT HONOUR AND A PLEASURE to welcome readers to the SPC Series.

The School of Psychotherapy and Counselling at Regent's College (SPC) is one of the largest and most widely respected psychotherapy, counselling and counselling psychology training institutes in the UK. The SPC Series published by Continuum marks a major development in the School's mission to initiate and develop novel perspectives centred upon the major topics of debate within the therapeutic professions so that their impact and influence upon the wider social community may be more adequately understood and assessed.

A brief overview of SPC

Although its origins lie in an innovative study programme developed by Antioch University, USA, in 1977, SPC has been in existence in its current form since 1990. SPC's MA in Psychotherapy and Counselling programme obtained British validation with City University in 1991. More recently, the MA in Existential Counselling Psychology obtained accreditation from the British Psychological Society. SPC was also the first UK institute to develop a research-based MPhil/PhD programme in Psychotherapy and Counselling, and this has been validated by City University since 1992. Largely on the impetus of its first Dean, Emmy van Deurzen, SPC became a full training and accrediting member of the United Kingdom Council for Psychotherapy (UKCP) and continues to maintain a strong and active presence in that organization through its Professional Members, many of whom also hold professional affiliations with the British Psychological Society (BPS), the British Association of Counselling and Psychotherapy (BACP), the Society for Existential Analysis (SEA) and the European Society for Communicative Psychotherapy (ESCP).

SPC's other programmes include: a Foundation Certificate in Psychotherapy and Counselling, Advanced Professional Diploma Programmes in Existential Psychotherapy and Integrative Psychotherapy, and a series of intensive Continuing Professional Development and related adjunct courses such as its innovative Legal and Family Mediation Programmes.

With the personal support of the President of Regent's College, Mrs Gillian Payne, SPC has recently established the Psychotherapy and Counselling Consultation Centre housed on the college campus which provides individual and group therapy for both private individuals and organizations.

As a unique centre for learning and professional training, SPC has consistently emphasized the comparative study of psychotherapeutic theories and techniques while paying careful and accurate attention to the philosophical assumptions underlying the theories being considered and the philosophical coherence of those theories to their practice-based standards and professional applications within a diversity of private and public settings. In particular, SPC fosters the development of faculty and graduates who think independently, are theoretically well informed and able skilfully and ethically to apply the methods of psychotherapy and counselling in practice, in the belief that knowledge advances through criticism and debate, rather than by uncritical adherence to received wisdom.

The integrative attitude of SPC

The underlying ethos upon which the whole of SPC's educational and training programme rests is its *integrative attitude*, which can be summarized as follows.

There exists a multitude of perspectives in current psychotherapeutic thought and practice, each of which expresses a particular philosophical viewpoint on an aspect of being human. No one single perspective or set of underlying values and assumptions is universally shared.

Given that a singular, or shared, view does not exist, SPC seeks to enable a learning environment which allows competing and diverse models to be considered both conceptually and experientially so that their areas of interface and divergence can be exposed, considered and clarified. This aim espouses the value of holding the tension between contrasting and often contradictory ideas, of 'playing with' their experiential possibilities and of allowing a paradoxical security which can 'live with' and at times even thrive in the absence of final and fixed truths.

SPC defines this aim as 'the integrative attitude' and has designed all of its courses so that its presence will challenge and stimulate all aspects of our students' and trainees' learning experience. SPC believes that this deliberate engagement with difference should be reflected in the manner in which the faculty relate to students, clients and colleagues at all levels. In such a way this attitude may be seen as the lived expression of the foundational ethos of SPC.

The SPC Series

The series evolved out of a number of highly encouraging and productive discussions between the Publishing Director at Continuum Books, Mr Robin Baird-Smith, and the present Academic Dean of SPC, Professor Ernesto Spinelli.

From the start, it was recognized that SPC, through its faculty and Professional Members, was in a unique position to provide a series of wide-ranging, accessible and pertinent texts intended to challenge, inspire and influence debate in a variety of issues and areas central to therapeutic enquiry. Further, SPC's focus and concern surrounding the ever more pervasive impact of therapeutic ideas and practices upon all sections of contemporary society highlighted the worth, if not necessity, of a series that could address key topics from an informed, critical and non-doctrinal perspective.

The publication of the first three texts in the series during 2001 marks the beginning of what is hoped will be a long and fruitful relationship between SPC and Continuum. More than that, there exists the hope that the series will become identified by professionals and public alike as an invaluable contributor to the advancement of psychotherapy and counselling as a vigorously self-critical, socially minded, and humane profession.

PROFESSOR ERNESTO SPINELLI
Series Editor

Notes on Contributors

Michael Jacobs is a leading figure in psychodynamic psychotherapy who, until January 2000, was director of the counselling and psychotherapy programme at the University of Leicester. Following early retirement he moved to Swanage in Dorset, which is his base as an independent consultant in psychotherapy and counselling. He has a small therapy and supervision practice, undertakes occasional teaching commitments, especially in the area of supervision, and lectures or runs workshops on a variety of topics. He continues to edit books in a number of different series, which often span different therapeutic orientations, and he still writes in the field of psychodynamic therapy and counselling, the area where he is best known. He is registered with UKCP, and is a Fellow of the British Association for Counselling and Psychotherapy, for which organization he chairs the Practice Development Committee. He is a member of the British Association for Psychoanalytic and Psychodynamic Supervision.

Windy Dryden is a world-renowned rational emotive behaviour therapist and is currently Professor of Counselling at Goldsmith's College, University of London. He is a Fellow of the British Association for Counselling and Psychotherapy and of the British Psychological Society. He is a major contributor to the literature on counselling and psychotherapy, having written or edited 124 books, and edited thirteen major book series in the area of counselling and psychotherapy.

Malcolm Parlett, a former experimental psychologist and then qualitative researcher, has put a lot of energy over a twenty-year period into explaining, promoting and practising gestalt psychotherapy in Britain. He is the founding editor of the *British Gestalt Journal* (since 1990); a co-founder and teaching and supervising member of the Gestalt Psychotherapy and Training Institute; and a Visiting Professor of Gestalt Psychotherapy at the University of Derby. In addition to gestalt teaching, in Britain and internationally, and his therapy practice (group and individual) and supervision, he works as an organizational consultant. He has written extensively about gestalt therapy, notably in developing 'field perspective' – central to present-day gestalt thinking and practice. This is the focus for a book which is in preparation.

Dorothy Rowe is an associate Fellow of the British Psychological Society. From 1972 to 1986 she was head of the North Lincolnshire Department of Clinical Psychology. Since she left the NHS she has been engaged in research, writing and teaching. Her research and writing have focused on the questions of how we create meaning and why we suffer. She is the author of twelve books and regularly gives lectures and runs workshops in the UK and internationally. Her books have received wide public acclaim; she is particularly well known for her books on depression and how to deal with it. She no longer practises as a therapist but follows the developments in the field of psychotherapy through her work both academically and in the media.

Miles Groth is a highly respected and eloquent spokesman of existential psychotherapy who is on the Faculty of Wagner College, Staten Island, New York. He trained as a psychoanalyst and continues to see patients in addition to teaching and writing. In May 1999 Dr Groth organized the first conference on existential psychotherapy to be held in New York since the late 1970s. He is a member of the Society for Existential Analysis, the American Philosophical Association and the American Heidegger Conference.

Anthony Stevens is one of the world's leading Jungian analysts and regards himself as in the 'classical' tradition; however, a number of other influences, among these being the work of John Bowlby, also contribute to his work. He has degrees in experimental psychology and, like Bowlby, believes that analytic theories and practices should be open to empirical verification. For the last ten years he has been actively engaged in exploring the links between Jung's archetypal hypothesis and developments in the new discipline of evolutionary psychiatry. He has published books and papers on this subject, on his own and in collaboration with the evolutionary psychiatrist John Price. He has now virtually retired from analytic practice and devotes his time to writing and teaching both in the UK and in Zurich, St Petersburg, the US and Canada. He is a member of the Royal College of Psychiatrists, a senior member of the Independent Group of Analytical Psychologists, and a member of the International Association of Analytical Psychologists.

John Rowan is a counsellor and psychotherapist in private practice in north-east London. His contributions to the explication of humanistic psychotherapies have deservedly gained the status of 'classic texts'. He teaches, supervises and facilitates groups at the Minster Centre in London, where he is also Link Tutor with Middlesex University. He is on the editorial boards of *Self & Society*, the *Journal of Humanistic Psychology*, the *Transpersonal Psychology Review* and the *Counselling Psychology Review*. He leads workshops on Creativity, Subpersonalities, Men's Consciousness and Transpersonal Psychology in a number of different countries. He has had twelve books published, as well as many chapters and papers in journals. He is a founder member of the UK Association for Humanistic Practitioners and sits on its Membership Committee. He is a Fellow of the British Psychological Society and

Deputy Chair of the Examination Board of the Division of Counselling Psychology. He is a Fellow of the British Association for Counselling and Psychotherapy.

Alvin Mahrer is Professor Emeritus, School of Psychology, University of Ottawa, Canada. Author of eleven books and over 200 publications, and recipient of the Distinguished Psychologist Award of the American Psychological Division of Psychotherapy, he is probably best known for his work in four areas. One is his comprehensive experiential psychology of human beings, personality and social change. A second is his experiential psychotherapy and method of having one's own experiential sessions. A third is his discovery-oriented approach to psychotherapy research. The fourth is his application of philosophy of science to the advancement of the field of psychotherapy.

Having introduced our contributors, it is only right that the editors say something about themselves:

Ernesto Spinelli is the author of numerous articles and texts dealing with various aspects of existential psychotherapy and phenomenological psychology. He is Professor of Psychotherapy, Counselling and Counselling Psychology at The School of Psychotherapy and Counselling, Regent's College, London, and is the editor of the new SPC Series of psychotherapy texts published by Continuum, of which this present book is among the first.

Sue Marshall is an integrative psychotherapist in private practice in East Sussex and Kent. She teaches on training courses at the Tunbridge Wells Counselling Centre and also works as a supervisor and runs workshops. She is a member of the Society for Existential Analysis and is accredited by the UKCP.

Embodied Theories: An Introductory Overview

Ernesto Spinelli and Sue Marshall

T HE INITIAL IMPETUS for this book originated in a fascinating passage recounted by Sigmund Freud in his autobiographical study (Freud, 1925). During one of his first meetings with the French neurologist, Jean Martin Charcot, the young Freud was stunned to hear him pronounce: *La theorie, c'est bon, mais ca n'empêche pas d'exister* ('Theory is fine, but that does not negate what exists'). It had occurred to us that, of the great diversity of factors that exists for all psychotherapists, the most directly accessible yet least considered is that of their current stance toward, and relationship with, their chosen theoretical model. More specifically, we were interested in addressing the general question of how psychotherapists' lived attitude toward their preferred model serves to shape not just what they do and who they present themselves as being when interacting with their clients, but also how it reflects and impacts upon their more general currently lived way of being and the varied attitudes and concerns which shape and inform it.

All therapists rely to a great extent upon their theoretical models in order to give meaning and purpose to their work with clients. If one were to ask a therapist what model or theoretical framework he or she subscribes to, it would be surprising not to be given a straightforward reply. Further, if that same therapist were to be asked to provide an outline of the preferred model's principal tenets and assumptions, one would expect that the task would not be experienced as being overly onerous or challenging. And, if one were to persist and ask the therapist how he or she came to be allied to that model, it is not unlikely that an autobiographical account specific to the question under consideration could be presented without too much difficulty. Indeed, various worthwhile and educative texts have already been written examining various representative therapists' personal journeys of discovery leading to their association with a particular model of psychotherapy (Dryden, 1992; Mullan, 1996).

What has not been sufficiently considered or written about, however, is how such representative therapists have subsequently come to interpret – and, likely re-interpret – their theoretical models from *an embodied standpoint*. If one's adopted theoretical approach can be likened to the clothes one wears with which to both cover and delineate the overall shape, contours and expressive potential of one's body, then our interest lies in questions that seek to address and explore such issues as: How does this theory 'fit' you? What sense of 'movement' does it allow, encourage or restrict? When you first came across it, was your initial reaction one of 'This is just what I had in mind and have been searching for for years!'? Or was it 'How odd and unusual! I wonder what I'd look like if I tried it on?' What parts or aspects or features of it do you continue to appreciate and treasure, feel irritated with or concerned by, or don't notice or pay attention to at all? All these questions, and many more that could be conjured up with relative ease, point to the overall concerns and focus of this text. Its primary aim is to provide a context through which various psychotherapists attempt to explore and communicate what and how it is for them to embody their chosen theory.

As such, the contributors have been encouraged, wherever possible, to avoid the more common approach of considering their theoretical model from a primarily abstract perspective designed to provide readers with a general outline of its most salient and unique characteristics. In much the same way, the authors have been asked to keep to a minimum the recounting of those parts of their autobiographies which seem pertinent to their development as practitioners or which have led them to the adoption of the model. Both these focus points, while undoubtedly interesting and deserving of analysis, serve to distance the account from its author either because, as in the first case, the emphasis lies on the abstract and general rather than upon the concrete and personal/specific; or because, as with the latter, it shifts the temporal focus toward the past rather than seeks to address that which is current in the author's lived experience.

Instead, the contributors have been presented with the task of addressing the issue of how they 'embody' the theories they practise; that is to say, they have been invited to write an account that attempts to examine those features and aspects of their chosen models which significantly and currently inform and clarify their professional lives as expert psychotherapists, as well as those aspects of their more personal lives which they are willing to disclose to public awareness and scrutiny.

But, the reader might well ask, why should we, and our contributors, concern ourselves with such questions? What makes them sufficiently significant that they should merit the interest of our authors and readers alike? In part, we could simply state that there exists something about the very enterprise of psychotherapy – perhaps as distinct from most, or all, other professions – that requires such unusual explorations. It seems, to us, to be something about 'the very nature of the beast' that deems it pertinent, if not necessary, to engage in these enquiries. On further reflection, however, this type of enquiry also seeks to address a broader, if no less relevant, set of concerns.

Psychotherapy has never been so popular nor as much in demand as it is today. Over the last decade, training programmes and academic courses in psychotherapy have increased dramatically in Britain, Australia and North America. In a similar fashion, both Britain and Australia have encouraged the development of various 'umbrella' organizations such as the United Kingdom Council for Psychotherapy (UKCP), the British Association for Counselling and Psychotherapy (BACP) and the Psychotherapy and Counselling Federation of Australia (PACFA). These organizations have begun to register and accredit psychotherapists and counsellors who fulfil specialist criteria for practice. In addition, the British Psychological Society (BPS), the Australian Psychological Society (APS) and both the American and Canadian Psychological Association (APA and CPA, respectively) maintain Divisions and Sections whose professional focus lies in the allied territories of psychotherapy and counselling psychology. Recent developments in Britain – mirroring, at least in part, those of their counterparts in North America and Australia – have moved to the point where it is highly likely that during the next few years the statutory 'licensing' or regulation of psychotherapeutic practitioners will become a reality.

At the same time, however, the 'boom' in psychotherapy has also generated wide-ranging concerns about the enterprise and its consequences – concerns which have focused principally upon instances of abuse (be they sexual, physical, financial and/or psychological) perpetrated by therapists upon their clients. More generally, the tendency – potential or otherwise – for both psychotherapists and their clients to assume that therapy alone can 'make things right' for people or, alternatively, that therapy alone can provide the means for serious and beneficial critical self-awareness and insight have been rightly criticized as being arrogant, dangerous and just plain stupid.

Much of the current 'backlash' against therapy seems to us to be in part a reaction to the presentation of psychotherapy as the panacea for all our psycho-social ills. This view of the profession is a deplorable misunderstanding and debasement of psychotherapy. For, rather than being about the attainment of certainty, security, 'perfect harmony' or whatever other final and fixed stance to life one might fantasize, psychotherapy, if anything, is geared toward the recognition that uncertainty and insecurity are 'part of the package' of living. The psychotherapeutic encounter, therefore, is but one means available in which to explore the experiential options individuals may have (which, admittedly, may be very few indeed in many instances), not only so that they may 'live with' the uncertainties and unknowns with which we are all confronted, but also that these 'givens' of life may even be exhilarating and joyous as well as frightening and painful.

All psychotherapists – ourselves included – act as representatives of a model or theory. However 'sensible' or 'way out' any one, or all of such models may reveal themselves to be, whether as a whole or in part, when their assumptions and hypotheses are more carefully considered, the current scientific research evidence which exists (whether its focus lies in either the exploration and clarification of variables within the psychotherapeutic process itself, or whether it is concerned with evidence-based outcome studies) remains both problematic and inconclusive. While it is almost certainly the case that, in general, psychotherapy is more likely to provoke beneficial rather than harmful outcomes, it is also the case that we continue to know next to nothing as to why such outcomes occur or what the most pertinent variables influencing such outcomes may be (Spinelli, 1994). Just as significantly (and, perhaps, more so) there exists a distinct lack of evidence to indicate that any one of the plethora of psychotherapeutic models is inherently superior to, or more likely to produce better outcomes than, any other. Such a current state of circumstances should not lead us to conclude that 'all models of psychotherapy are of equal worth and beneficial impact'. Rather, all that can be stated at present is that we just don't know whether some models are superior or inferior to others with regard to their outcomes. In part, this is likely to be due to the complexity of quantitative and qualitative variables that are present in any psychotherapeutic encounter which, in themselves, make research a difficult, if not 'impossible' enterprise (Kline, 1992; Roth and Fonagy, 1996).

Although such disturbing questions are by no means new to

the profession, we have sought to consider their impact and implications by contextualizing them within what we believe is an original and worthwhile investigative structure whose basis rests in the broader attempt to discover whether there is anything in the way that psychotherapists themselves interact with and make personal sense of their theories that might serve to provide potentially valuable new perspectives on these recurring problems.

We start from the premise that since psychotherapists in some way do live out the theories which they espouse, then the attempt to explore how and in what ways they do this, which aspects of their theories play a significant part in their daily lives, which do not and, in general, how their theories inform and challenge the therapists' way of being and living their current lives both professionally and from a personal context, may prove to provide future research with useful and novel information. This may clarify just what there may be about psychotherapy that, as yet, has not been sufficiently delineated and understood as 'necessary conditions' to desired outcomes.

Embodied Theories sets out to explore the various ways in which a therapist can be a living expression, or embodiment, of his or her chosen theoretical model. In approaching several major representatives and internationally renowned practitioners of psychotherapy and inviting them to write about the ways in which they each live their chosen theory, our hope is to discern a number of possible recurring themes that may be elaborated further in subsequent research analyses.

Specifically, the questions we posed for each of our contributors to consider and address were:

- How do you currently give expression to your chosen theory from the context of your own currently lived personal and professional experience?
- In what specific ways, if any, does your chosen theoretical model impact itself upon your life – both professionally and in general?

- How, if at all, does your chosen model significantly inform, guide and/or clarify those aspects of your life that remain of particular interest and/or concern to you?
- What aspects of the theory influence and resonate within your way of being and understanding yourself and your relations with others? What aspects bear little, or no, relevance to your life as currently lived and experienced?
- To what extent, if at all, has your chosen model challenged views, attitudes, beliefs and behaviours that you had previously maintained with regard to your practice of psychotherapy, and with regard to your personal life?
- What would you have been like as a psychotherapist, or as a person, if you had not come across your model?

Those readers who maintain an interest in the varied approaches to research will likely have noted the distinctly phenomenological influence that underpins our questions. As a primary contributor to qualitative research methods, phenomenological investigations place central emphasis upon descriptive analyses whose intent is to tease out descriptively focused statements designed to illuminate a wide range of 'meaning possibilities' that can emerge within a structured focus of inquiry (Colaizzi, 1978). It seemed to us that this approach was the most adequate, and potentially rewarding, through which to address the issues that interested us, our contributors and, hopefully, the readers of this book.

On reflection, the task we asked our contributors to undertake was far more arduous and challenging (and, perhaps, more arrogant) than we had initially suspected. That they have all responded so openly and engagingly to it should be seen primarily as an outcome of their own willingness to bring an unusual degree of openness to a profession whose more typical insistence upon its practitioners' maintenance of an attitude requiring mystery and concealment remains the subject of much debate and satire.

As editors, we were both well aware, from our own initial

attempts to pursue the enterprise that, once initiated, it was highly likely that each would present original – perhaps even surprising – 'lived interpretations' of his or her relationship to a specific theoretical model. In turn, we suspected, this novel perspective might well serve to clarify, de-mystify and certainly 'humanize' the relationship between psychotherapists and their theoretical models in ways which patients or clients, students, and, indeed, most practitioners are likely to encounter in a more detached, abstract form.

Following this introductory chapter, the text is divided into eight chapters, each dedicated to one particular 'living theory' as embodied by an expert representative. The closing chapter of the book then attempts to consider some of the more pertinent and intriguing issues and themes that emerge from the authors' accounts.

The models under consideration have been selected on the basis of their distinctive features and import to the world of contemporary psychotherapy. These include analytic models (such as psychodynamic psychotherapy and analytical psychology), humanistic models (such as gestalt psychotherapy and humanistic–integrative psychotherapy), cognitive–behavioural models (such as rational emotive behaviour therapy), experiential models (such as personal construct psychotherapy and experiential psychotherapy) and existential–phenomenological models (such as existential psychotherapy).

Of course, a great many more specific or derivative models remain to be considered. While no single text of this sort could ever hope to cover all, or even the greater percentage of the 400-plus currently existing models and theories, our initial attempts sought to gain the interest of as wide-ranging a selection of approaches as could be reasonably represented. While we are unequivocally pleased with both the quality and diversity of approaches represented here, and hold every expectation that our readers will be similarly satisfied, nonetheless we must also acknowledge some degree of disappointment with regard to two significant – and obvious – factors.

First, it had been our hope to maintain a more even gender balance among our contributors. As it stands, however, seven of the eight contributions are by male psychotherapists. All that we can say with regard to this lop-sidedness is that we tried long and hard to attract the attention of several well-known and respected female psychotherapists, but, in the end, failed to gain their sufficient interest in the enterprise. Why this should be remains, frankly, something of a mystery to us. One possible answer may begin to emerge via the consideration of the second factor: the reticence to participate expressed by the great majority of psychoanalytic practitioners whom we approached. While some were willing enough to express the view that the aims of our project compromised their model's insistence upon the maintenance of the practitioner's anonymity, it must also be acknowledged that a substantial proportion of the analysts whom we approached did not respond to our invitation; or, to put it perhaps more accurately, chose to respond by way of silence. While it is not our intent to either question or criticize either of these stances, it remains the case that, as the greatest proportion of the analysts whom we approached were also women, this may go some way toward clarifying the gender bias that no reader is likely to miss.

Nonetheless, such limitations and considerations should not diminish the value and power of the eight contributions that make up the body of this text. We are immensely grateful to each of our authors for the thought and effort that he or she has put into this enterprise. The feeling of excitement and interest that was generated for the editors with the appearance and subsequent reading of each individual paper cannot be easily conveyed to the reader; we leave you to discover what we hope will be something very much akin to it.

Finally, it remains to be stated that, on the basis of their comments to us, all of the contributors found the experience of writing their chapter to be both challenging and revealing of the great many ways, both overt and subtle, that their present stance toward, and relationship with, their chosen model informs, clarifies, and, at times, even contradicts their intended ways of being, whether in their professional lives as psychotherapists or in their wider personal and interpersonal relations with themselves, others and the world in general.

We would suggest to our readers that they might find their reading of this text to be most rewarding – be it professionally or personally – if, prior to entering the lived worlds of our contributors as recounted in their chapters, they first set aside some time to consider their own responses to the questions we have posed. In this way, we believe, the possibilities and challenges of critical engagement with their own preferred theoretical models will convey in a more directly experienced fashion the unexpected merit to be found through embodied investigation.

References

Colaizzi, P. F. (1978) 'Psychological research as the phenomenologist views it', in R. S. Valle and M. King (eds) *Existential-Phenomenological Alternatives for Psychology*. New York: Oxford University Press.

Dryden, W. (1992) *Hard-Earned Lessons from Counselling in Action*. London: Sage.

Freud, S. (1925) *An Autobiographical Study* (trans. J. Strachey). New York: W. W. Norton & Co., 1963.

Kline, P. (1992) 'Problems of methodology in studies of psychotherapy', in W. Dryden and C. Feltham (eds) *Psychotherapy and its Discontents*. Milton Keynes: Open University Press.

Mullan, B. (1996) *Therapists on Therapy*. London: Free Association Books.

Roth, A. and Fonagy, P. (1996) *What Works for Whom: A Critical Review of Psychotherapy Research*. New York: Guilford Press.

Spinelli, E. (1994) *Demystifying Therapy*. London: Constable.

2 | Reflections (Psychodynamic Psychotherapy)

Michael Jacobs

P SYCHODYNAMIC PSYCHOTHERAPY takes its lead
from psychoanalysis, although it is important that I
identify myself as a psychodynamic psychotherapist rather than
as a psychoanalytic psychotherapist. The reasons for this will
become clearer as this chapter unfolds. Nevertheless, my roots
as a therapist are in that discipline, therefore I approach the
questions asked by the editors from a psychoanalytic perspective: it was where I began my studies and my practice, and it
continues to provide much of the inspiration for my thinking.

Psychoanalysis is nothing unless it is understood as a
dynamic model, and indeed the history of psychoanalysis has a
particular dynamic which it has sometimes failed to examine.
From a dynamic perspective, various aspects of the individual
personality, and of human relationships generally, interweave to
form a whole complex (I use the word in its commonly understood sense), in which, despite the best efforts to identify a
typology or to hypothesize a structure to the mind, it seems to
me impossible to disentangle the depths of the psyche. It is
therefore similarly difficult to disentangle three particular
aspects which contribute to my sense of my self. Consequently
while I am invited to write about the way in which psychodynamic psychotherapy makes an impact upon me, I cannot
but also wonder how much I (that is my own personality) have
influenced the way in which I interpret and understand psychodynamic psychotherapy. Furthermore, the body of writing

and practice which has obviously been a major influence upon me has itself been influenced (sometimes without it being fully recognized) both for the writer and for me the reader by the milieu in which it initially flowered, and in which, in different cultures and different historical times, it has continued to be construed.

I therefore ask myself a number of questions which need to be linked in order to present the fullest picture: not just what is the impact of psychoanalytic and psychodynamic thinking and practice upon me, but what impact do I myself make upon the way I have understood and developed my understanding of psychodynamic theory and practice? Not just how does my theoretical perspective challenge me and my ideas, but in what ways do I challenge my chosen theory? Not just what sort of person has my theory made me, but what sort of theory has been attractive to me as a person? And extending these questions further, I also have to ask how much the world and the society in which I live, as well as the times through which I have already lived, have explicitly and implicitly influenced those theories, and how much they have influenced me in the way I approach those theories.

If this seems a complicated way of approaching what may appear initially to be straightforward questions, the very elements which interweave all suggest that this is inevitable. Put simply at this point, my own personality does not permit me to accept that there is much (at least in the discipline of psychotherapy) which is clear-cut; my chosen theory also emphasizes the impossibility of ever knowing more than a small part of how human beings function; and the cultural milieu with which I find myself most in tune, the postmodern, leads me to doubt the permanence of much of the knowledge in my discipline, constructed as it is within a particular segment of a particular society at a particular time.

Freud, the progenitor of my chosen theory, did and did not feel the same. For him psychoanalysis was (apparently) more important than himself, and his autobiography is much more an exposition of the history of his ideas than of himself: he is at one and the same time keen that his theories should be remembered rather than himself; and yet of course he rightly identifies his life with the development of those theories. As he says in the first paragraph of that autobiography (Freud, 1925), he had already written much about himself, because many of the examples in his work (e.g. the dreams in *The Interpretation of Dreams*) reveal more about him than the casual reader ever realizes.

Similarly, he did and yet did not recognize the importance of his cultural milieu. That he did is witnessed by his speculative studies of society and civilization in some of his later work (Freud, 1921, 1930) and their relation both to collective and individual psychological health; and in the links he clearly saw between the expectations of society and the health of many of his patients (Freud, 1908). Yet his emphasis on phantasy as playing as important a role as actual events in the aetiology of hysteria set in train an exaggerated concern for the inner world in psychoanalysis generally, and a neglect both of the political dimension and actual history, collective or personal.

We may therefore legitimately ask whether psychoanalysis was discovered by Freud, or whether psychoanalysis enabled Freud to discover himself. Returning to myself, I may also legitimately ask whether it was me who discovered the value of psychoanalytic theories for myself, or whether they discovered me. Has the way in which I have developed as an individual over the many years since first reading Freud been the result of my involvement in psychodynamic thinking and practice, or has my interpretation of theory and practice been as a result of other influences upon me, both in society at large, and in the more intimate personal relationships in which I have been involved?

It is therefore impossible for me to separate out the past and the present, or the interplay of the many factors that have impinged upon me in my life. The reader would, I think, expect this of someone with a psychodynamic perspective; and indeed

I find considerable support for this position in different aspects of the theories which interest me. Notice that I now write 'theories' and not 'theory'. Psychoanalytic literature is so rich in theories that I can both draw upon what seems important to me, and also put to one side those ideas which seem untenable, or more possibly not yet demonstrable to me in my experience of clients or myself; or which appear irrelevant or unintelligible in my present state of mind. Whether it is intellectual incomprehension or unconscious resistance that prevents me from grasping some of the ideas I come across in psychoanalytic literature, I cannot tell.

Those concepts in psychoanalytic writing which clarify the complex interactions which have formed me are valuable to me, then, in helping me understand where I come from and how I am as a therapist and as a private individual. Freud's structural account of the psyche, the tri-partite division of ego, id and super-ego, appealed to me at first: here was a way of visualizing the pulls and pressures within me. It was, and still is, a model which has a simplicity which clarifies conflicts and dynamics for clients: 'a part of you would like . . . a part of me says . . .'. Those early, relatively straightforward Freudian principles still retain their power to explain and relieve the inner conflicts of troubled minds. I try not to forget what insight this initially gave me when working with people now, even though my personal position now perceives personality formation and structure as infinitely more complex.

It is the concepts of 'internal objects' (although as with much of psychoanalytic literature I do not like the actual term), and of the infinite set of movements throughout life between 'projection' and 'introjection', that best express this relationship between myself, my psychodynamic theory and practice, and the milieu in which I live and work. What have I put into others and what have they put into me? What have I taken in from others, and what have they taken in from me? And – increasing the complexity – what do I take from others that I have already put into them, or receive from them that they have already perceived in me? This way of thinking operates at a deeper level in me than the intellect alone. Indeed, it would be arrogant for me to suggest that intellectually I understand much more than the concept itself: the many layers of inter-penetrating of person to person make it impossible to understand precisely what comes from where, whom or when.

Another, more accessible way of describing the same ever-present phenomenon of inter-relating is Winnicott's phrase 'there is no such thing as a baby' (Winnicott, 1964). Intellectu-ally his idea stretches reality too far, but the image of the mother and baby co-dependent upon one another is one that appeals to me. Indeed, the responsiveness of adult and child to each other has indeed been demonstrated in video studies, and begs the question of who initiates any exchange of feelings. In relation-ships, whether in the family, the consulting room or indeed in the lecture theatre, we and those whom we are with are like a hall of reflecting mirrors: 'mirror' is an image with which I feel more at ease than 'screen', because the last thing we are, whether in private or as therapists, is 'a blank screen', even those who consciously adopt and espouse such a pose.

When I am listening to a client I try to listen both with these many mirrors in mind, and yet also without any desire to make perfect sense of what I see and hear. Bion's phrase 'without memory or desire' (Bion, 1967) is one I came across long after I had originally trained, although I doubt if it would have made any real sense to me had I heard of it earlier. I had to reach a point where Bion's words described what I was already experi-encing in my work before I could value them: it was the advice of someone who had similarly found this was the better way for him to work, and who had put it into words for me. I try not to look for psychopathology, for causes, for explanations or solu-tions. All I have read and studied, or learned through supervision and my own therapy and continuing self-analysis, and all I have gained through years of seeing many different clients – all this is best kept in the background, like one huge data bank of memories, ideas and emotions. Sooner or later a penny drops, or a connection appears, and an idea can be tested. But I expect the idea to lead to another, and another – and if it does not, it was either the wrong idea or an idea before its time.

It was not always so: and here I need to return to my opening paragraphs, in order to ask whether it was psychoanalysis that discovered me, or me psychoanalysis. In the first place, historical circumstances need to be taken into account. In the late 1960s there was less choice of trainings than now: apart from psychoanalysis, there seemed only to be behavioural therapy (too mechanistic by far for my artistic temperament) and American West Coast therapies (too emotional and too physical for my reserved and private self). I need not here go into the accidental events that led me away from an initial flirtation with Jung to the more readily understood Freud; nor from one profession (the Church) to that which has become my principal career. What is important is to recognize that there were accidents of history; a particular person at a particular point who suggested a particular direction. I do not believe that any of these were fore-ordained, although in one sense they may have been accidental events waiting to happen, inasmuch as I clearly responded to some cues, and not to others.

Psychoanalysis appealed for a variety of reasons. I had been working in a caring profession – therapy and counselling offered the same opportunities. Psychoanalysis had a substantial body of knowledge, one which provided an alternative to the theological knowledge that had hitherto sustained my intellectual interest and my emotional fervour, but which had begun to lose its viability and its veracity for me. It asked similar questions, if phrased rather differently, to those that had clearly appealed to me in religion. Freud too had wanted to resolve 'something of the riddles of the world' (Freud, 1927), just as I had been previously engaged in trying to solve the riddles of existence and the universe, and in a rather more microcosmic way pursued the same quest.

What I did not see at the time, but has become so much

more obvious to me since, is that psychoanalysis also appealed because it was cultic like the Church (as indeed were behaviour therapy or the encounter groups and Esalen-type alternatives of the time). Therapists and counsellors often feel passionate about their therapeutic schools and positions, and I was no exception. Psychoanalysis beckoned with a type of certainty. The reader will realize the contrast between this early position and my current one. It had its dogmas; indeed, as I began to discover, it had its creeds, and in some societies woe betide the person who tried to step outside them. It had a whole set of moral views – although they are called 'psychopathology' rather than 'sin'. I could 'analyse' people rather than hear their confessions. I could help relieve their guilt, rather than pronounce forgiveness. I could achieve a new kind of status, because as the status of clergy declined, the admiration of counsellors and therapists came in.

I exaggerate slightly, but in order to make the point. Psychoanalysis suited me: it fitted, if not quite like a glove, at least enough to support my personal characteristics. Indeed, what is ironical is that I was leaving the Church because it was dogmatic, intolerant and narrow in much of its public thinking, and I felt that it had no place for my more radical, questioning and independent mind. That I should then have allied myself to psychoanalysis is now not at all surprising, given the power of 'the return of the repressed': this is one of Freud's greatest discoveries which I still hold true, and which sometimes makes me think that very little changes – even as a result of years of therapy. In some ways I went from the frying pan into the fire. But not completely, because I did change, at least in my conscious mind, and I like to think those changes seeped a little lower into a layer or two of my unconscious. The 'return of the repressed' also applied to my free-thinking spirit. If I was on the one hand rather conformist – public school, Oxford and the Church – on the other I had always been uncomfortable with the conformity of others and of institutions: a careful rebel at school, somewhat radical in the Church, and now independent within psychotherapy, and hence able to reach a point where I could see how psychoanalysis might entrap me. I was fortunate, because I did not ever undertake a prescribed 'training' as such, and fortunate too that I worked 100 miles from London. Fortunate because training with a psychoanalytic society or association – especially in London – tends to produce a mindset which finds it difficult to question accepted wisdom, both of theory and practice; or makes it very difficult to voice this within what remains a largely conservative profession.

When I then consider how much the theory that I chose to study and practise has changed and modified me, I find it difficult to disentangle the different ways in which it has freed me from a wish for certainty (invariably unfulfilled before it mattered less), from a preoccupation with duty and guilt, from a Protestant work ethic (without lessening my enjoyment of the task) and from an anxiety about openness and intimacy. Conversely I wonder how far psychoanalytic theory and practice have in fact sustained those characteristics in me, under the guise of being a psychodynamic therapist, and through what such a therapist should believe. For example, when I first began to practise, 'not knowing' made me extremely anxious; although the accepted therapist stance of saying little and turning questions back to the client enabled me to mask that lack of knowledge, and perhaps to hide much of my anxiety, so as not (I trust) to disturb the client. Contentment with uncertainty, or even excitement that where there is uncertainty there is always the possibility of finding something new, came much later: and with it the discovery not just of Bion's 'without memory or desire', but also of Winnicott's profound ability to tolerate gaps in his knowledge, and his emphasis on the creativity of 'the space between'. His notion of inner space, and the 'for ever silent' central self out of which 'communication naturally arises' (Winnicott, 1965) have become an essential 'credo' for me, without having to make it, as once I might have done, into a creed. But I had to be ready for Winnicott, and then Bion, and I am not sure that it was my elected theory that made me so. What it did, however, when the time was right, was to provide me with the resources to support the position to which I was moving. Subsequently dipping into the vast treasury of writing from a psychoanalytic perspective has also enabled me to find that there are indeed many other analysts and therapists who appear to think along similar lines. Psychoanalysis has its pockets of conservatism indeed, and it has its fair share of rather cloned practitioners who are afraid to question what they have been taught, and what their personal therapist has modelled to them by way of practice. It also has others (and I come across many of these) who wait for permission to express their doubts and uncertainties, not having learned that it is safe to do so in their training.

Was my view of the dogmatism and certainties of psycho-analysis my own projection, or was it something which I internalized from some of my experiences of analysts? It is the interplay of these different forces that provides the most complete answer, and what proportion of projection and introjection there was does not matter to me. What is important is to remind myself periodically that this is so, because the need to deny is always present, and the psychoanalytic concept of denial is also extremely relevant.

I take another example of the way in which psychoanalysis initially met my needs. Like the priest in the pulpit, the thera-pist is placed at a distance from parishioner or patient. This place is partly professional, and I have no wish to see it or prac-tise it in any other way than by being utterly professional. I have rarely known clients in other roles, as friend or colleague, nor have I any particular wish to. I prefer to see myself as someone who may play a vital part at a particular stage of a person's life, but who can be let go of, except in memory and as some hope-fully good enough internalized figure in their innermost life. I value this distancing and discreteness in psychodynamic therapy. But at the same time the chosen stance in my early days protected me from becoming too involved; not so much in the transference and counter-transference, which can be very useful concepts, if sometimes ways of denying the reality of the therapist–client relationship, but in terms of sharing the ordinary human response. This was strange, because it was not the example set by my own therapist, himself a leading analyst. It was a projection of mine on to the conventions of technique which was not without foundation (because the literature is full of it), but one which then suited me. I made this projection without testing (or indeed seeing with my own eyes) whether this was really the way psychoanalytic therapists behave. My projection supported my personal need. And for a while in those early days I became much more withdrawn socially, as if the observing, careful, non-disclosing therapist had leaked into my life outside the consulting room. I think now this was because I was needing to find a new identity as a therapist in place of being a priest, and therefore needed to hide in my shell until that identity was firm enough to risk its fuller exposure.

Yet here too I have changed, withdrawing perhaps the projections, and internalizing other models of how to relate as a therapist. I have reversed the process and allowed my more social skills to leak into being a therapist. Was it my elected theory that enabled this to happen? Perhaps so, although I can think of other explanations. One is that I began to take up a teaching role again, one of the aspects of being a priest which I had profoundly missed when my working life became restricted to the four walls of my consulting room: the pulpit had no place there, or it took more subtle forms. Teaching counselling restored the extravert side to me, one which had always been present previously in drama, in leadership roles at school and university, in teaching as well as preaching in the church. There was then a danger that as a therapist I would begin to 'teach' my clients, much as I see Freud instructing his patients, and Mrs Klein telling her child patients what their games really meant. Being a teacher has at times interfered with my therapeutic style: one client told me that I tended to make the same interpretation three times in slightly different words! But being a therapist has largely enhanced my teaching, making me so much more interested in enabling students to find out what is relevant for them, rather than insisting that I know what they should understand about a particular concept or approach. And teaching has enhanced my therapy, making me more questioning of my hypotheses and my way of being.

This change in style has come with confidence; in knowing that it is fine to be myself, as long as I am careful to check whether what I would like to express will, on the balance of probabilities, not disturb or distract the client. It has also come, as so much else I have described, with discovering that others before me have been through this quest for their own identity as a psychotherapist. Lomas (1973, 1999) I discovered and indeed met with early on, although it was some fifteen years later that I really took notice of his own search for authenticity, and particularly his own embodiment of being 'ordinary'. Like him, I had to break away from conformity in order to discover my own identity as a therapist, although since taking inspiration from Lomas I have found numerous examples of analysts who to varying degrees are clearly just as present as themselves in their sessions as they are as therapists – Sigmund Freud (in his practice if not in his written advice to practitioners), Anna Freud (see Couch, 1995), Ferenczi (see Dupont, 1995) and Searles (1965), to name the most obvious. Being 'ordinary' has become an important facet for me: being ordinary cannot be a goal, neither is it something one can set out to achieve. It is especially important to try to remain so when one's public image tends toward being seen as in some way elevated.

I have no wish in my private life to be seen only as a therapist. There is of course a tendency for much psychoanalytic writing to analyse (what more would one expect!) and even to pathologize, and this can make for an uncomfortable way of perceiving others, including oneself. The question is sometimes asked, often when meeting strangers socially and revealing one's occupation, 'Does that mean you can analyse people?' – meaning 'me?'! And yet at one stage I think (with horror now) that this may have been true. As someone steeped in psychodynamic theory I can still readily phrase my perception of others in psycho-speak, especially when required to do so in various professional situations. It is sometimes difficult not to look back on people met in the course of the day, and to comment upon them using psychodynamic concepts, even if the comments are not necessarily critical. That may be a feature of being married to another therapist, and drawing upon a common language that can be readily understood; but it is also a mind-set which does not easily rest.

Yet there has been a significant change over the years. One of the features of the psychoanalytic culture which I most abhor is what I might call 'displaced sadism'. It appears to make some psychoanalytic therapists, teachers and supervisors hypercritical. Whether or not they show this to their patients I do not know, but I see considerable evidence of it in the way some students and supervisees experience those who teach them. That hyper-critical, hyperanalytic attitude is one I knew myself, in relation to myself perhaps more than my clients, and in relation to other forms of therapy which did not appear to fit the model I had chosen for myself. Whether it is the return of my questioning spirit, or the influence of the *rapprochement* I perceive taking place across many of the therapies; whether it is the softening that comes with maturing years, or whether it is in reaction to so much persecutory teaching and supervision that I hear about from those who come to study with me: what has changed is that I make my analytic comments about myself and others now with a lighter touch, without the persecutory edge, trying to empathize and understand, rather than to label and put down.

I believe and hope that this is true of my personal life too. There is a tolerance which I have achieved, but not at the cost of desiring the highest standards for myself and others. Tolerance is not something that I perceive to be obvious in the psychoanalytic world, and the splits within psychoanalysis, including the perpetuation of divisions in psychoanalytic therapy in Britain, are a witness to the fact that many others prefer to put their emphasis on standards rather than on tolerance. If I am intolerant, it is of this in-fighting, which may not only be true of psychoanalysis: the Jungians have their own splits (Casement, 1995), and I imagine there must be tensions between the different humanistic therapies too. But the therapeutic 'family' which I have chosen seems preoccupied with internal quarrels, and this would distress me were I not still sufficiently individualistic to say 'a plague on all your houses', and where necessary go my own way. I am fortunate to have initiated a psychodynamic psychotherapy training, and to belong to a psychodynamic association which I helped found, which can, in many ways, be described as tailor made.

My other major concern about psychoanalytic and psychodynamic therapy is that it is too inward looking. It is, I accept, reasonable to expect a psychological therapy to concentrate upon the psyche. But there has been over many years, as I indicated at the start of this chapter, more interest in phantasy than in historical event, and so much value placed upon the concept of change in the individual psyche, that there has been far too little attention paid to the external circumstances which continue to constrict development. I have to be careful not to be too sweeping in this criticism: psychoanalytic group therapy has always been of interest to me, but time and expense have prevented me from pursuing it further. Here there is concern for the social, and for inter-relatedness, which helps correct the individualism of much therapy. Therapeutic communities, and the more radical ideas of R. D. Laing (1965) and those who have followed him, complement the picture. Samuels and others have promoted the social and political dimension of psychotherapy, thankfully across orientations. But generally psychoanalysis has been very narrow in its actual impact, concerned more with its own politics than with the wider world; and even if it has been enormously influential in intellectual circles as well as popular culture, it often appears determined to follow Freud in a greater interest in researching the psyche than in being genuinely therapeutic: by which I mean reaching out to the mass of emotional distress at large.

I am not generally political as a therapist, or even as a private individual, even though I take an interest in politics – both of the profession and in what sometimes seems more like the 'real world'. Perhaps it is therefore unfair to chide psychodynamic therapists for not being different. However, I am active in trying to make therapy more available, and am uncomfortable with the élitism of much psychoanalytic therapy. The almost inherent conservatism of psychoanalysis has too long held out against developing widely accessible forms of treatment, despite some practitioners leading the way in offering therapy to the general public, in developing short-term therapy (e.g. Malan and Osimo, 1992; Molnos, 1995), and in adapting the model for a much wider clientele. My sense of public service has been a major element in my life, and found expression in the Church, continued in developing a university counselling service, and then saw me co-founding a counselling centre for the general public regardless of ability to pay. Although I may be known and appreciated as an accessible writer on psychodynamic therapy and counselling, for myself my greatest achievements have been in helping to make psychodynamic therapy and counselling accessible to those who for one reason or another, including cost as well as prejudice about age or social background, have been excluded from it.

Essentially I have been drawn to the practical: although I have found many of the questions raised by psychoanalytic theory fascinating, those which I ultimately pursue are those which resonate with my experience, and are rooted in practice. It is why my writing is geared to being pragmatic rather than speculative. I may write about theory, but I am not essentially a theorist. For one who likes to get things done, and done well, psychotherapy seems a strange occupation in which to have found myself. Results there are, but they can be a long time coming, and they are not always permanent. I can sometimes be cynical about the depth of real change: perhaps people, including myself, adapt rather than radically alter themselves.

Before I was able to be more obviously productive through

teaching, writing and organizing projects, there was an important part of me which in practising therapy alone experienced frustration at the narrowness of my concerns. I may have been fortunate, but I have also been active in seizing the opportunities to develop my interests in psychodynamic psychotherapy outside the consulting room. Had I not, I suspect being a psychodynamic practitioner day in and day out might have crushed me. My marriage and family always represented a different world outside therapy, which in some ways provided that essential separate environment, although it has been my second marriage, where my psychodynamic work has been so much more fully understood, that has provided the greater integration of work and the rest of my life. In a partnership with many other interests than therapy there is a natural movement between being in the discipline, and getting away from it. Psychotherapy is in any case only one major area of discourse for me. There are others which are just as important: the novel, poetry and music, for example, which might be said to approach the same issues from different perspectives. If I have always valued the arts, and indeed the natural world, increasing years make me even more appreciative of these alternatives to psychotherapy. Fortunately some psychoanalysts are also deeply interested in these areas, even the natural world (see Searles, 1960), and this makes for convenient ways of combining my different interests. I now prefer the writer who illustrates psychodynamic concepts from literature (e.g. Britton, 1998) to what once fascinated me, the writer who psychoanalyses the text (e.g. Freud, 1907).

And what if I had not become a psychodynamic therapist? What would I be like as a person and practitioner now? The question cannot be answered because it is essentially a speculative one. It is not that I could not have been anything else, perhaps even a therapist of a different school. There have always been some initiatives which have not been effective, but if they had they might have led to me being in a completely different occupation and place. What sort of person I would have been, had the accidents of history been different, I cannot tell: although I am sure that in some ways I would have been different, and in other more inward ways I would have been the same. That, after all, is what my psychodynamic perspective attests to, that what is laid down in the early years of life has a profound influence upon the growing child and adult. As I once used to express in metaphysical theological language, the accidents would have been different, but the substance would be the same.

References

Bion, W. R. (1967) 'Notes on memory and desire', *Psychoanalytic Forum*, 2, 272–3, 279–80.

Britton, R. (1998) *Belief and Imagination: Explorations in Psychoanalysis*. London: Routledge.

Casement, A. (1995) 'A brief history of Jungian splits in the United Kingdom', *Journal of Analytical Psychology*, 40, 327–42.

Couch, A. S. (1995) 'Anna Freud's adult psychoanalytic technique: a defence of classical analysis', *International Journal of Psychoanalysis*, 76(1), 153–71.

Dupont, J. (ed.) (1995) *The Clinical Diary of Sándor Ferenczi*. Cambridge, MA: Harvard University Press.

Freud, S. (1907) *Delusions and Dreams in Jensen's Gradiva*. Penguin Freud Library, Vol. 14. London: Penguin Books.

Freud, S. (1908) *'Civilized' Sexual Morality and Modern Nervous Illness*. Penguin Freud Library, Vol. 12. London: Penguin Books.

Freud, S. (1921) *Group Psychology and the Analysis of the Ego*. Penguin Freud Library, Vol. 12. London: Penguin Books.

Freud, S. (1925) *An Autobiographical Study*. Penguin Freud Library, Vol. 15. London: Penguin Books.

Freud, S. (1927) *Postscript to 'The Question of Lay Analysis'*. Penguin Freud Library, Vol. 15. London: Penguin Books.

Freud, S. (1930) *Civilization and Its Discontents*. Penguin Freud Library, Vol. 12. London: Penguin Books.

Laing, R. D. (1965) *The Divided Self*. Harmondsworth: Penguin.

Lomas, P. (1973) *True and False Experience*. London: Allen Lane (reprinted 1994, New Brunswick: Transaction Publishers).

Lomas, P. (1999) *Doing Good? Psychotherapy Out of its Depth*. Oxford:

Oxford University Press.

Malan, D. H. and Osimo, F. (1992) *Psychodynamics, Training and Outcome in Brief Psychotherapy.* Oxford: Butterworth/Heinemann.

Molnos, A. (1995) *A Question of Time: Essentials of Brief Dynamic Psychotherapy.* London: Karnac Books.

Searles, H. (1960) *The Nonhuman Environment in Normal Development and in Schizophrenia.* New York: International Universities Press.

Searles, H. (1965) *Collected Papers on Schizophrenia and Related Subjects.* London: Hogarth Press.

Winnicott, D. W. (1964) *The Child, the Family and the Outside World.* London: Penguin Books.

Winnicott, D. W. (1965) *The Maturational Processes and the Facilitating Environment: Studies in the Theory of Emotional Development.* London: Hogarth Press.

3 | How Rational Am I? Self-help Using Rational Emotive Behaviour Therapy

Windy Dryden

I FIRST RECEIVED TRAINING in rational emotive behaviour therapy (REBT) in 1977 and have practised it ever since. Before that I was trained in person-centred therapy and had some training in psychodynamic therapy, but neither of these therapeutic approaches resonated with me as much as REBT did, and still does. In this chapter I will consider:

1. Why I resonate personally with REBT theory and practice.
2. How I implement REBT successfully in my personal and professional life.
3. In which areas I struggle implementing REBT in my life.
4. Where REBT is not relevant in my life.

Let me stress at the outset that my account (and, if I may venture, that of my colleagues) is bound to be influenced by *post-hoc* rationalizations, and will therefore provide a more coherent narrative than is likely to be the case in reality. It will also be coloured by what I choose to disclose. On this latter point, my self-disclosure will not be as full as you, the reader, may wish. Since I do not know in advance how my revelations will be used in future, I will disclose as much as I feel comfortable about my professional life and particularly about my personal life.

While this chapter is decidedly not a chapter on the theory and practice of REBT, if you know very little about this approach then what I have to say will not mean that much to you. Consequently, let me first provide a thumbnail sketch of REBT so that you can understand to what extent REBT is for me an embodied theory.

The essence of REBT

Rational emotive behaviour therapy is an approach that is best placed within the cognitive–behavioural tradition of psychotherapy. It is based on a particular view of emotional disturbance which is summed up in a slightly altered version of a famous dictum, the original of which is attributed to Epictetus: people are disturbed not by things, but by their rigid and extreme views of things. In REBT theory, these views are known as irrational beliefs and take the form of demands (e.g. 'I must be loved by significant others'), awfulizing beliefs (e.g. 'It would be the end of the world if I was not loved by significant others'), low frustration tolerance (LFT) beliefs (e.g. 'I couldn't bear it if I was not loved by significant others') and depreciation beliefs where you depreciate yourself (e.g. 'If I am not loved by significant others then this proves that I am unlovable'), depreciate others (e.g. 'If significant others do not love me then they are no good') or depreciate the world/life conditions (e.g. 'The world is no good for allowing me not to be loved by significant others').

The basic goal of REBT is to help clients to change these irrational beliefs to a healthier set of rational beliefs which are flexible and non-extreme in nature. These take the form of full preferences (e.g. 'I want to be loved by significant others, but I don't have to be'), anti-awfulizing beliefs (e.g. 'It would be bad if I was not loved by significant others, but it wouldn't be the end of the world'), high frustration tolerance (HFT) beliefs (e.g. 'It would be difficult for me to bear not being loved by significant others, but I would be able to bear it and it would be worth bearing') and acceptance beliefs where you accept your-self (e.g. 'If I am not loved by significant others then this would not prove that I am unlovable. It proves that I am a fallible human being who is deprived of the love that I want, but do not need'), accept others (e.g. 'If significant others do not love me then they are fallible human beings who are depriving me of the love that I want, but do not need. They are not bad people') or accept the world/life conditions (e.g. 'The world is a complex place where good things happen, bad things happen – like me being deprived of the love that I want, but do not need – and neutral things happen. It is not a bad place just because I am not loved by significant others').

REBT is a structured, educational, active-directive approach to therapy where, within the context of a good thera-peutic relationship, clients are taught a range of cognitive, imaginal, behavioural and emotive techniques. The purpose of these techniques is to enable them to internalize and integrate rational beliefs into their belief system so that they make a real difference to the way that clients feel, think and act both intrapsychically and interpersonally. In this sense, REBT encourages clients to adopt a self-help philosophy. For more details on the principles and practice of REBT, consult Ellis (1994).

Why I resonate personally with REBT theory and practice

Although I was originally trained in person-centred counselling and psychodynamic therapy, I did not resonate personally with either of these approaches. However, I did resonate with both the major theoretical principles of REBT and its practical ethos. For example, years before I became a counsellor I helped myself overcome my anxiety about the possibility of stammer-ing in public by implementing what was in essence a typical REBT treatment approach. I heard Michael Bentine on the radio talk about how he coped with his stammer by convincing himself: 'If I stammer, I stammer, too bad.' I took this rational statement and made it more evocative by convincing myself: 'If I stammer, I stammer, fuck it!' Then I rehearsed this belief while using every opportunity to speak up in public without modifying what I said so that I did not avoid words over which I was highly likely to stammer. In doing so, I lost much of the anxiety that I experienced about speaking in public and, as a consequence of this anxiety reduction, I stammered less. I believe this example shows that I naturally resonated with the following:

1. That one can help oneself by actively confronting one's fears (the principle of behavioural change).
2. That one can influence the way one feels by changing one's beliefs (the principle of cognitive change).
3. That one can help oneself without being in counselling or psychotherapy (the principle of self-help).
4. That one can help oneself by changing current factors that maintain one's psychological problems without necessarily exploring the past (the principle of present centredness).

The question is: why do I resonate with these and other REBT principles? The short and uninspiring answer to this question is that REBT suits my temperament and character. These are factors which are largely biologically based, which I am easily drawn to and find natural to actualize. These factors are both intrapsychic and interpersonal in nature. Let me then explore some of the elements of my temperamentally based character and show how these lead me to be particularly suited to using REBT in my personal and professional life.

Activity level
I have always had quite a high activity level. I am easily drawn to areas where I can actively do something to help myself and others and where I can be actively involved in personally meaningful projects like writing professional and self-help material.

When I reflect in depth on my experiences of personal therapy which have been largely psychodynamic in nature (and which fall outside of the scope of this chapter), I conclude that one of the main reasons why I found these frustrating and largely unhelpful experiences was that they didn't help me to do something active to help myself. Also, when I am not actively involved in personally meaningful projects, I get restless and easily bored. Thus, I have made several decisions to stop writing which I have broken because I miss this activity. So I have learned to go with my internal flow and give up making promises I really don't want, in my heart of hearts, to keep.

Self-discipline
Without wanting to blow my own trumpet, I will admit that I have rarely had a problem with self-discipline. Again this is largely due to my (in my view, largely innate) obsessive-compulsive traits. Thus, when I make up my mind to do something, I am very likely to persist until I have done it or until it becomes clear that I will not be able to do it. I almost always keep to deadlines and more often than not, I do things well before the deadline (like this chapter). Yes, I learned the value of self-discipline from my parents, but have very little difficulty putting it into practice. In short, it 'goes with' the grain of my temperament. In contrast, I learned the value of eating slowly from my parents, but have great difficulty doing so. This seems to 'go against' my temperamental grain. REBT stresses the need for humans to be self-disciplined and to view this as a lifelong project. I resonate with this view and have no problem with it (unlike the majority of my clients who initially view this with something akin to horror).

Self-reliance
Whenever I have had an emotional problem I have been drawn to help myself to overcome this problem. In the past I have failed to do so only because I lacked the knowledge of what to do to help myself, not because I have sought to be helped by

others. I have, of course, sought help from others, but these help-seeking episodes have rarely borne substantial fruit largely because they failed to provide me with a sound and sensible course of psychological action to follow which would help me to overcome these problems. When I discovered REBT in 1977, it was as if I had 'come home' so to speak, so comfortable did I find it as a way of overcoming emotional problems. Yes, being an only child helped by providing me with an environmental context where I could easily express my tendency towards self-help, but I firmly hold that it did not originate this tendency. While many only children are natural self-helpers, many are not.

Cognitive and philosophic orientation

I mentioned above that I have a high activity level. I am also very much at home in the cognitive modality. Little wonder that I resonate with a cognitive–behavioural approach such as REBT. But why do I resonate more with REBT than with other cognitive–behavioural approaches? One of the reasons is that REBT has a decided philosophic emphasis. Far more than other cognitive–behavioural therapy (CBT) approaches, REBT outlines a philosophy of healthy living that is both realistic (e.g. it acknowledges that humans have a predisposition toward irrationality as well as toward rationality) and optimistic (i.e. it argues that humans can transcend even tremendous tragedy with their spirit shaken, but not broken). It is the combination of the realistic and optimistic that appeals so much to me and helps explain why I never truly resonated with person-centred philosophy (too idealistic for my realistic side) and psychodynamic philosophy (too pessimistic for my optimistic side). Other CBT approaches are either philosophically indifferent or philosophically poorly developed.

Humour

While others may disagree, I consider that I have always had a good sense of humour and fully agree with Albert Ellis (1987) who has said that psychological disturbance involves taking oneself, others and life *too* seriously. Not that I laugh *in*appropriately at myself, but I regard aspects of life that others cherish such as status, reputation and social standing as relatively unimportant. Thus, I am generally amused rather than angry when I hear of some rumour or other about myself that from time to time circulates in the counselling/therapy rumour mill. Even when I received a verbal warning at work for using profanity in the classroom (not, I hasten to add, for swearing *at* any of my students), I was amused as well as pissed off when contemplating the ease with which one or two of my students disturbed themselves about my language. Although this episode and its aftermath period had its trials, it also had its funny side as college wrestled with attempting to specify occasions when it is admissible to swear in class (apparently when you drop a heavy object on your foot and the expletive is involuntary). For me REBT is the Heineken of therapies, reaching humorous parts of myself that other therapies cannot reach.

Non-religious, anti-mystical orientation
I am also drawn to REBT because it resonates with my non-religious, anti-mystical side. While a number of REBT therapists have a religious faith, the theory does not encourage a 'faith unfounded on fact' view of the world and takes a decided stance against mystical, transpersonal ideas. The idea of a 'New Age' REBT is as likely as 'kosher bacon'. This suits me as I have never believed in God, reasoning quite early in my life that if there is a deity, why on earth (or heaven!) would he, she or it create Lot's wife a fallible human being and then turn her into a pillar of salt for showing her fallibility? No, I am an ethical humanist by persuasion and easily resonate with this aspect of REBT.

Lone pioneer
Finally, I am drawn to REBT because it is not popular (certainly not in Britain anyway). I am, I believe, Britain's leading proponent of REBT and have been beavering away to make it

more accessible on this island. There is a part of me that resonates to my role as a lone pioneer struggling to make REBT's voice heard in a crowded market-place dominated by humanistic and psychodynamic practitioners. That part of me doesn't want REBT to be too successful. If it were, I would lose my lone pioneer role. While I don't make too much of this dynamic, it does exist in me.

Is there anything within REBT theory which resonates to this idea of the 'lone pioneer'? Yes, but in a way that is different from how this dynamic operates in me. I am referring here to the idea that it is important to pursue ideas which are personally meaningful even if it means incurring wrath and disapproval from others. REBT theory holds that it is self-defeating to believe that it is essential to be approved of by others; doing so will lead one to abandon one's pursuit of enduring meaning in favour of receiving approval which is transitory. I note that Albert Ellis himself pursued the promulgation of REBT in the face of severe criticism and personal abuse from the field in the mid-1950s and beyond. In those days he was a lone pioneer. But he did not waver from presenting his ideas whenever he could, because he did not need the approval of his peers.

Having speculated on why I am so drawn to REBT, let me go on to consider how I apply it in my life.

How I have implemented REBT successfully in my personal and professional life

The proof of the pudding of any therapeutic approach is in its eating. So how successful have I been in applying the principles of REBT to my personal and professional life? I think, in my biased view, that I have done so quite successfully and here are some examples of Dryden-centred REBT in action.

1. I practised the REBT principle of unconditional self-acceptance (Dryden, 1999) after I left my lecturing job at Aston University in 1983 and I failed to get any of the 54 jobs I applied for over a two-year period. 'That must have been very depressing for you', people said when I told them about this period of my life. 'Actually, it wasn't,' I replied, 'because I had 54 job rejections and no self-rejections.'

2. I implemented a high frustration tolerance (HFT) philosophy once I learned that I had high cholesterol by adopting a low-fat, low-cholesterol diet and forgoing many of the high-fat foods that I love. Whenever I am tempted to break this diet, I acknowledge that I am tempted, I recognize that I would like the high-fat food, but show myself that I don't need what I want. Not that I deprive myself of all high-fat foods. I have four squares of chocolate every Friday! I have also exercised five times a week for years now and again implement a similar HFT philosophy in doing so. Most of the time I don't want to get up and exercise, preferring to remain in bed, but I push myself to get up while reminding myself that I can stand the discomfort of getting up and it is worth it to me to do so.

3. Whenever I am in writing mode (which is fairly often) I resolve to write 500 words a day and very often exceed this figure. What if I'm not in the mood? In such cases, I remind myself that I don't need to be in the mood in order to write and push myself to get going. Most of the time I get in the mood after I have started, and even if I don't get myself in the mood I write anyway. In this way, I live a lifestyle which is rarely affected by procrastination (Dryden, 2000).

These three examples show that I am pretty adept at persisting through adversity as long as there is a point in doing so. As I said before, I believe that I have a temperament which facilitates this process, but I still have to push myself when the going gets tough.

Another good example of how I used REBT in action to

cope with adversity concerns my reaction to the following episode. A number of years ago I wrote a self-help book entitled *Overcoming Shame*. As usual I finished this book ahead of schedule and effected a transfer of files from a memory card attached to my trusty Amstrad NC200 to a floppy disk. Unfortunately I wiped the files from the memory card before checking that they had been successfully transferred to the floppy disk and, yes, you've guessed it, the floppy was blank. I had lost the whole book because, as I discovered later, I had used one full stop too many while naming each of the files. Initially I went berserk, started throwing things around and calling myself all the names under the sun. I was furious with the world for inventing fucking stupid things called computers, and with myself for being such a fucking stupid individual. Dear reader, please don't be offended by my language. If you are a counsellor or therapist, hopefully you should not be shocked by profanity, and I'm trying to give you an honest account of my inner dialogue at that time.

Well, you might argue this doesn't seem very rational; throwing things about and cursing the world and yourself for making a mistake – a mistake albeit with serious consequences – but a mistake nonetheless. But let me finish the story. This inner- and outer-directed tirade only lasted for about a minute, for I stopped myself in mid-rant, acknowledged to myself that I was unhealthily angry, accepted myself for adding self-inflicted insult to injury, and reminded myself forcefully that my anger wasn't helping me to solve my practical problem.

After I had calmed myself down, I went on to tackle my self-depreciation. Yes, I reasoned, I had acted stupidly, but no, I was not a stupid individual. I was and remain a fallible human being capable of creativity such as writing a book on overcoming shame, and of a stupid act such as failing to institute simple checks that I 'know' I should ideally have done. That's human beings for you, I reminded myself, fallible and capable of fucking-up (I am using the actual words that I used with myself at the time because they did help me).

After accepting myself for my grave error, I then tackled my awfulizing belief. Yes, I acknowledged, the consequences of my stupidity were serious: six months of hard slog down the drain or into the ether, or wherever my damned data went. This was very bad, but awful, terrible or the end of the world? Hardly. I would always remember the incident, to be sure, but would I, I wondered, refer to this incident on my deathbed as the worst thing that happened to me, let alone the worst thing that *could* have happened to me? Definitely not, I exclaimed to myself. Yes, it's bad that I lost the book. I value my time, and the thought of devoting a good deal of it with nothing substantial to show at the end is difficult for me to tolerate. But losing the book is hardly awful and I can definitely tolerate it and, furthermore, doing so will help me to make the important decision concerning whether to rewrite the book or to give up on the project. Rehearsing these rational beliefs helped me to feel the constructive emotions of annoyance and disappointment rather than the unconstructive emotions of unhealthy anger and depression that I would have experienced over time if I hadn't identified, challenged and changed my irrational beliefs. These constructive emotions helped me to weigh up the pros and cons of rewriting the book, which I decided to do without complaint after I had concluded that this was what I wanted to do and that to do so was in my long-term interests. The result was the book *Overcoming Shame* (Dryden, 1997) in which I discussed this entire challenging but growthful episode.

The final area in which I have used REBT successfully again concerns self-acceptance. The REBT concept of self-acceptance is a profound one (Dryden, 1999). It encourages people to accept themselves for being fallible, unique organisms. I have already touched on how I used REBT to accept myself as a fallible human being for my angry reaction to losing an entire manuscript. Here I briefly want to focus on self-acceptance for being unique. I have a number of idiosyncratic interests. Earlier in life I might not have pursued some of them because I would have believed that a person of my intelligence and professional standing shouldn't be pursuing such interests (e.g. watching boxing and the soaps on television). Now I see that I am a person of complex diversity; that there is no need for me to attempt to fool myself into thinking that I am other than multi-dimensional. So, these days, I am more in tune with my 'real' self and hardly inclined at all to pigeon-hole myself.

Areas where I struggle to implement REBT in my life

Are there any areas where I struggle to implement REBT in my life? There most certainly are. Perhaps the area of personal difficulty that I struggle with the most is unhealthy anger. I very easily anger myself when others frustrate me in significant ways, when others get away with acting badly or when they receive advantages that (in my view) they do not deserve. I am well aware that when I make myself unhealthily angry I am holding strong demands about being significantly frustrated and about interpersonal unfairness, but I have great difficulty giving up these demands. I do so in the end, but it involves a great deal of forceful REBT-inspired effort on my part and often the effects only last until the next relevant episode.

Why do I struggle so much with unhealthy anger? Because in my view I have a strong genetic predisposition towards this unconstructive negative emotion. Virtually all the males on my father's side of the family have been quick to anger and this can be traced back over several generations. It's not that I fail to see clearly that unhealthy anger has far more costs than benefits, because I see this most clearly. It's just that on occasion (and sadly these occasions are becoming more frequent, the older I get), I experience a powerful push towards unhealthy anger. I am never violent and I do calm down fairly quickly, partly naturally and partly through using my REBT skills with myself very forcefully. But this doesn't stop me from making myself angry very easily the next time some significant frustration or unfairness impinges upon my personal domain. I usually express my angry feelings verbally, but very occasionally I have been known to throw the odd piece of furniture around (but not in the direction of another human)!

Another area in which I struggle to use REBT effectively may seem superficial, but it is important to me. As far back as I can remember, I have bolted down my food, often finishing a dish before the person I am lunching or dining with has half-eaten theirs. I find this habit frustrating because I would like to have a long lingering meal and I am sure that eating more slowly would have a beneficial effect on my digestion. Again, my felt experience is that I am struggling with a habit with a genetic loading behind it, but whether or not this is the case, it takes a great deal of mindful REBT-inspired effort for me to slow down my eating. Even though I may have done this on one occasion, the very next time I eat, I may well mindlessly wolf down my food again if I am not vigilant.

As I said earlier, I like to be active and I find it fairly easy to be self-disciplined. This is just as well because I do struggle when I have too much work to do. When this happens – and typically it occurs when I come back from holiday and have a great deal of post to deal with both at home and at work – I am vulnerable to stress because I try to deal with the pile of letters *too* quickly. Here, my implicit belief is that I have to be on top of things all the time and I can't stand it if I'm not. If I do not mindfully tell myself that I don't have to be on top of things at all times and that I can stand to work methodically rather than quickly, I will tend to try mindlessly to do several things at once and get myself quite stressed. This need to get things out of the way quickly has also led me on occasion to make impulsive decisions which I have later come to regret.

On thinking carefully about the issues that I struggle with, it seems to me that I find it much easier to tolerate the discomfort that is associated with making an effort and being disciplined than the more acute discomfort associated with not being on top of things and being frustrated.

Where REBT is not relevant in my life

REBT is a therapeutic approach which, like other therapies, has two basic goals: to help overcome disturbance and to promote psychological growth (Mahrer, 1967). In this chapter I have concentrated on showing how I have used REBT (or struggled to use it) to overcome psychological disturbance, although I have also alluded to how I have used it to promote growth in the areas of self-discipline and self-acceptance. However, there are numerous other areas where REBT is not relevant in my life. Thus it has little or no impact on my political leanings and it has no bearing on what I find involving or interesting. For example, I enjoy football and am a season-ticket holder at Arsenal. Does REBT have an influence here? Decidedly not. It would be relevant if I disturbed myself about the grim fact that Manchester United beat us 2–1 at home this season (1999–2000). But I didn't, so it doesn't. Unlike psychoanalysis, REBT does not seek to take a position on a range of social, political and cultural issues. Rather, it sticks with what it is good at: offering a perspective on psychological disturbance and a set of procedures to help people overcome their disturbance and move toward psychological health.

In this chapter, I have outlined why I resonate with REBT, how I have used it successfully in helping me to overcome my own disturbance and to further my own development, and I have discussed areas where I struggle to use REBT effectively. In all other areas of my life, REBT has little or no relevance – and that, in my opinion, is as it should be.

References

Dryden, W. (1997) *Overcoming Shame*. London: Sheldon.
Dryden, W. (1999) *How to Accept Yourself*. London: Sheldon.
Dryden, W. (2000) *Overcoming Procrastination*. London: Sheldon.
Ellis, A. (1987) 'The use of rational humorous songs in psychotherapy', in W. F. Fry, Jr, and W. A. Salameh (eds), *Handbook of Humor*

in Psychotherapy: Advances in the Clinical Use of Humor. Sarasota, FL: Professional Resource Exchange.

Ellis, A. (1994) *Reason and Emotion in Psychotherapy* (revised and expanded edition). New York: Birch Lane Press.

Mahrer, A. R. (ed.) (1967) *The Goals of Psychotherapy.* New York: Appleton Century Crofts.

4 | On Being Present at One's Own Life (Gestalt Psychotherapy)

Malcolm Parlett

I

I have just come in from walking by the river below my house, to begin writing. I have notes next to me, accumulated since last summer, when the editors' invitation arrived, to write this chapter. I sit drinking tea; I consider how to begin – and realize I have done so already.

I notice I am sitting and typing, and yet when I stop and attend more closely to myself, I realize I am not altogether 'here' – either in this room or ready to begin. I am still outside. Strong mental images persist, like an aroma or echo: the trees newly stripped of leaves, the bright day and cold air, the gurgling and swishing sounds of the river, and the sensations registered within my wellington boots as I waded through shallow, fast-flowing water.

Writing about it now (I notice) collects and organizes the memory – integrates it – and helps to 'close the gestalt' (of the river walk). By attending to the 'what is' of my present consciousness, I am better able to focus on the here and now reality, involving the computer screen, my thoughts, beginning this chapter.

Intense observation and an almost Proustian interest in the flow of awareness are, of course, hallmarks of the gestalt approach (Perls *et al.*, 1951; Yontef, 1993; Parlett and Hemming, 1996a). In logging immediate thoughts and sensations, I am practising the core *phenomenological* discipline (like pianists play scales or athletes exercise). I am also beginning to respond to the questions put to me by the editors. How has the gestalt approach impacted me personally? How do I give expression to the theory? How does it inform my life?

Well, one of the things I try to do is remain 'in the present' – i.e. to stay in touch with my unfolding experience as it happens. It is all too easy to depart from the flow of immediate sensuous reality and disappear into thoughts, images, rehearsings, worries, fragments of memory – that ongoing mixture of free association and conversation with self, conducted at a sub-vocal (or sub-sub-vocal) level, which has the capacity to fill minds interminably. We can remain in this realm of consciousness (or rather semi-unconsciousness) for long periods – witness those times when we have driven long distances along familiar routes and have only 'woken up' when we arrived. 'How did I get here?' we ask.

Gestalt – not unlike some forms of Buddhist meditation – provides a means for interrupting the flow of self-talk, inviting us to return to 'now', 'here', 'the actual', in order to be 'more present'. Thereby, individuals can learn to notice and capture subtle feeling states that easily go unnoticed. They register themselves as alive physical beings; sensing, moving and feeling. They are ready to engage fully with others. In gestalt therapy there is value placed on this state of enhanced present awareness, as I shall make clear.

As I sit writing I am also conscious, as many a writer is, of the people who will read these sentences. Private jottings will not do: in reality I am engaged in two-way communicating. Evoking different images of whom the audience comprises – for instance, editors, or other psychotherapists, or gestalt trainees – subtly changes how I write, and what I write about. I am also dimly aware of the other writers in the collection, even if I do not know them personally or what they are writing about. Nothing happens without a context, no 'figure' without a 'ground'. And both together constitute the 'field' of my experience – in this case the emerging sentences and the background contexts into which they fit. The *field perspective* calls for paying exquisite attention to framing, co-regulation and contexts of experience.

To put it another way, I am attending to the 'contact boundary' (in gestalt terms) between my world and your world – my fingers tapping, the print on the page, your eyes moving, and so on. You and me, reader and writer, are meeting, here on this page. I can imagine you as a flesh and blood person, another being, a reader, just as you will have some image, however vague, of me the writer. Whatever the form of human meeting, or *dialogue*, there is some sense of felt connection. Here, this can be enhanced or diminished, according to how I write and your own degree of interest in what I am writing about. To reach you here, I want to bring my gestalt experience to you afresh – like fish dripping from the sea, rather than warmed-up fish slices from a packet.

You may have noticed I have italicized three terms above, the three legs on which present-day gestalt therapy stands: *phenomenology*, the *field perspective*, and *dialogue* (Resnick and Parlett, 1995). Together, these principles identify the approach: they are its *sine qua non*. I shall return to them.

2

There are now several points, I realize – all germane to writing about my experience as a gestalt specialist – that belong near the beginning.

First, a thought about what 'embodied theory' means, as seen from a gestalt perspective. To embody a theory, to the point that it 'becomes second nature', is the mark of an experienced specialist in any field. In assimilating gestalt theory, however, even beginning trainees are called on to begin embodying what they are learning. It has to be personally applied – often at a life-changing level – or it is hardly 'known' at all. This is because the 'theory' imbibed is more a philosophical world-view, or a way of thinking and perceiving, than it is a psychological or explanatory-type theory about, say, the causes of neurosis. Gestalt cannot be learned from books or lectures, any more than can throwing pots on a wheel or skiing.

To acquire the specific gestalt 'outlook' (including present-centredness, what it means to 'attend to the whole field', etc.) one must do more than gain familiarity with the various concepts, diagnostic terms and clinical terminology in use. As distillations of the gestalt outlook, they require first-hand knowledge of the phenomena to which they refer; i.e. the non-conceptual experiences alluded to. Otherwise they remain sterile and abstract, rather than directly owned. Words like 'contact', 'awareness', 'need', 'support' and 'process' are especially tricky, because while appearing simple and familiar, each is in fact steeped in specialist meaning.

A second point also relates to what gestaltists 'know'. Laura Perls (one of the founders) once said that 'in gestalt therapy there are as many styles as there are therapists and patients'. Gestalt therapy is not an orthodoxy: it is (or at least was intended to be) a wide-ranging, inventive, flexible approach, in which, she continues, 'a therapist applies himself in and to a situation with whatever life experience and professional skills have become assimilated and integrated as his background . . . He continually surprises not only his patients and groups, but also himself' (Perls, L., 1992). In other words, individuality and personal artistry are championed. Although some of the original anarchistic flourish has been compromised, and gestalt therapy has become altogether 'safer' (in several senses of the word) over the years, the assumption still holds: that every gestalt therapist achieves an individual integration. Each works in unique ways. Similarly, what I write here is not a party line. I speak for myself alone.

The third point is that none of us stands still, nor do therapy approaches. There have been many developments in psychotherapy and the gestalt community over the last half-century (Parlett and Hemming, 1996b). Inevitably, my own appreciation of gestalt philosophy has evolved over the 24 years since I first encountered it. The chapter I am writing in 1999 is different from what I would have written even two years ago, let alone in 1989 or 1979. Even a few months ago I would not be writing the same as now.

3

It is now evening time on the same day. Supper sizzles in the kitchen nearby. There is an air of stillness in the house. I sit quietly, looking back on what I have written so far. I am aware of a measure of discomfort about the last section.

Central to the lived, embodied experience of gestalt therapy is attending to the *aesthetics* of experience. Actions, events and life happenings of every kind (from cooking paella to arguing with a friend to organizing a funeral) differ in *gestalt qualities* – for instance, their roundedness and completeness, how 'balanced' they seem overall, and whether or not they have integrity, beauty, vitality.

Thus a 'felt discomfort', of the kind I am feeling at the moment about the last section, is attended to as a signal of departure from a satisfying *gestalt*. There is an in-built human sensibility (or 'sense-ability'), to notice the discordant note, the omission, misprint, or discrepancy from expectation; and also there is some sense of natural urgency to put right, complete, or fulfil what was ill-formed, unfinished, or askew.

My concern here, about the previous section, is because it feels lopsided. I may have given you the impression that gestalt has no settled structure, agreed procedures, or community influence on separate practitioners – that 'anything goes'. Such an impression would be wrong. For sure, there are differing schools of thought, local and national traditions, and pre-dictable arguments between traditionalists and revisionists. Yet there are recognizable continuities as well – theoretical, philo-sophical, methodological – which define the approach as a distinctive school of thought and practice. There is collective similarity as well as individual difference.

Several things bind us together as a community of professionals. For a start, we have to contend with some unfortunate yet prevalent stereotypes. No, I explain for the umpteenth time, gestalt therapy is *not* confined to some of Fritz Perls' techniques (like talking to sub-personalities or others represented by empty chairs). Nor is gestalt psychotherapy ultra-challenging and shame-inducing (at least as practised by the vast majority of us today). Nor is it focused on inducing emotional release. No, it is not always done in groups; and, yes, it definitely can be successfully applied in long-term therapy with personality-disordered clients. It would take too long here to discuss the misperceptions and how they arose and still survive today. Their continuance, however, is discouraging.

Gestalt practitioners also report remarkable similarity between people in their initial exposure to gestalt work. After they get over the 'culture shock' of encountering present-centredness and interpersonal directness, they get very excited by these features of the approach. They comment on the usefulness of the abilities, and the recognizable reality of its central ideas.

Obviously, there are other similarities between gestalt therapists: after all, we share the same 'brand'. Gestalt (like many other specialist approaches) is a minority therapy – that is, its practitioners are few relative to the community of psychotherapists generally. Yet it has made a mark. While the gestalt community has historically failed to propagate its approach widely, its influence (gestaltists comfort themselves by thinking) has been greater than generally recognized. Thus, current trauma-recovery work is pre-figured exactly in established gestalt methods; and the 'real' relationship in therapy has been a cornerstone of gestalt therapy for decades. Claims to intellectual copyright may be justified, but they also encourage a ghetto mentality, especially when linked to the widespread incidence of the simplistic stereotypes described earlier.

Gestalt psychotherapists, over the last twenty years, have been busy seeking to redress imbalances of earlier days, establishing organizations, promoting more effectively what they do and stand for, and writing much more than their predecessors did. The situation today is encouraging. World-wide there are more training courses, national associations, new books, international journals, conferences and meetings than ever before.

Although there have been many changes – and I have been involved in a number of them personally, partly through editing an international gestalt journal – the reality is that gestalt psychotherapy as a profession has a continuing ambivalence towards institutionalizing itself. Anarchistic leanings persist. We recall (somewhat wistfully) the bohemian nature of its beginnings. We are conscious of how the necessity for a flexible methodology runs counter to trends that, for instance, insist on protocols. In this way and others, we are aware of how its radical subjectivity contradicts certain modernist assumptions that persist. In two of the countries where gestalt therapy formerly flourished – the USA and Germany – there has been steep decline. In both cases the community of gestalt specialists was unable to compromise with state or insurance requirements, either because they could not, or would not philosophically.

I mention some of the tensions within the gestalt therapy community and profession because I am inevitably part of the community; I am affected by the tensions personally. I have embodied not just the theory but the professional field as well, with its hopes, enthusiasms, disappointments, and its resilient confidence in the worth of the approach. Even allowing for its minority status (or perhaps partly because of it) I derive satisfaction from feeling part of the collective experience. I realize, as I write this, how many colleagues are also friends, some very close ones. I notice I feel warmed and heartened.

4

Reading the last paragraph of the previous section leads me to another thought concerning friendship. One of the most common experiences among members of the gestalt community is that we enjoy ourselves when together (in this respect, obviously we are not alone). Being able to have good connections does not mean that gestaltists avoid the difficult politics that afflict (it seems) all psychotherapy groupings: we do not. However, the central discipline of 'the now', which everyone has also learned, means that tensions, hostilities and other unfinished business are more likely to get sorted rather than left to sour relations indefinitely.

There is a prevailing sense of upholding 'freedom to be oneself'. I believe this has a lot to do with members of the gestalt community having participated many times in groups, whether for therapy or training purposes. Either in, or around, these groups people have encountered openness and intimacy, self-expression and emotional honesty. In groups, even if the going is tough and heavy at times, there is also a spirit of child-like playfulness that is never far away. And I believe this orientation to a rich group life exists as a kind of 'folk memory' that can be (and is) reconstituted in other settings, especially with those who have shared common training experiences.

Having mentioned the powerful and satisfying nature of many gestalt therapy groups, I realize how much they continue to be part of my year-long cycle. I have come round to favouring group over individual therapy as my method of choice, and each year I orchestrate and run a number of groups – some ongoing, some short-term and intensive. Some of the atmosphere created in them spills into the rest of my life.

What groups provide, in terms of the culture usually developed within them, are conditions which seem all too rare in a world that is increasingly fragmented, individualized and cynical. A sense of communal experience, of mutual acceptance, of honouring both the serious and the comical, all make for a rare degree of fulfilment. They exist in sharp contrast to everyday patterns of communication on offer in our society, where reactions are often fear-based or self-protective, avoidance of contact is endemic, and neurotic conventions go unchallenged simply through being widespread. I often come away from gestalt group experiences feeling inspired. They re-affirm a sense of optimism about what is possible between human beings – that is, provided that coherent field conditions, attention to phenomenological process and a spirit of dialogue are all in place.

Of course (I add later) there are opposite trends as well. Attending to polarities and the 'shadow' side – to use a Jungian term – is intrinsic to a gestalt viewpoint. So it is also true, in the debit column, as it were, that the whole culture of group-life and seeking fullness of experience with others does not neces-sarily make for enhanced 'fit' with the mainstream of society. Sometimes, too, there have been destructive group processes which were never transformed, including (sadly) some within training centres between staff.

Overall, though, in all gestalt work, and in groups particu-larly, the attention to the aesthetic criteria alerts one both to what is present and to what is missing in many everyday situa-tions. Part of what a committed gestaltist acquires over time is a 'nose' for departures from wholeness, or interruptions to the flow of live events unfolding. I find (as other group psychother-apists of any 'brand' must do too) that I am hyper-attuned to noticing such things as the precise moment when a meeting begins to go 'pear-shaped', or when a performance is anti-climactic, or a protestation is not convincing. What is under-played, energy-reducing, contact-breaking, or plain absent, is attended to as a matter of course. Drawing on my implicit models or aesthetic criteria in this way – so central to the subtle phenomenological and intersubjective work of therapy with individuals – obviously spills over into non-professional life as well.

5

I return to this account two weeks later. As I sit down to write, I pause. Just as in any open-ended gestalt therapy session, group or individual, I am allowing space at the beginning, a time of staying quiet, of noticing what emerges as 'figural'. What is it, I ask, that stands out as figure against the ground of other matters in my conscious life – the present task, and all the rest of my experience this Sunday morning late in November?

What stands out first, today, is to make the point again: gestalt investigation begins with 'what is' – the immediate reality, phenomenologically given. It may not be what is expected or wanted; and it may soon be set aside, as one decides to follow another project or need. However, to ignore what is immediate and first given is almost to violate a fundamental axiom, that there is a certain unpremeditated organization of the present field that deserves to be respected. Often there are costs in ignoring what spontaneously arises.

What next stands out for me this morning, as a topic to write about, is the *holism* of gestalt therapy. It is another example of a taken-for-granted way of my viewing the world which derives from gestalt and is altogether assimilated now as my own. It is central to gestalt thinking that what is mentally or emotionally experienced is also knowable in visceral, somatic terms. Embodiment refers to a specific, literal process. Talking to a gestalt colleague yesterday, she reported intense back pain. It related (she thought) to her 'emotional state'. As she focused her awareness on the actual sensations in her back, moving her attention between these and her associations, and followed her unfolding experience, she connected progressively more and more to the circumstances of her present life, and also began to feel relief.

A holistic gestalt self-investigation of this kind includes attending to the flow of bodily energy (or 'chi'). This morning, even before waking, I realized how restless I was feeling – an unsettled energy. My partner is away this weekend and I thrashed around half-asleep knowing at least that I was not disturbing anyone. On waking more fully I was interested in a departing dream, which I briefly worked on, gestalt-style, to see if it would throw light on what I was restless about.

The kinds of dreamwork I do with myself include the following: I partially re-enter the dream state, if I can; I notice the physical 'felt sense' (Gendlin, 1981) that accompanies the dream. I pay it close attention and notice how it evolves and clarifies. At times I may 'become' parts of the dream and replay it from the points of view of other characters or dream elements. I imagine additions, subtractions and extensions; and I 'listen' throughout to what connections with my present life arrive in awareness. I ask myself: 'What am I being told by this dream?' or 'What have I been avoiding?' Sometimes I write the dream down and work on it more formally. Most mornings I run a kind of rough check and do some at least of the above. In noticing what nutrients are missing from my 'life-diet', I respect dreams as invaluable.

Similarly, much can be discovered by investigating somatic experience. Sometimes, especially when I am feeling unsettled or restless, I may simply begin to move, to 'listen to' my body with more attention than usual. This morning I spent half an hour moving and stretching spontaneously, breathing more deeply, and noticing as I did so what feelings and awarenesses arrived. There was no great 'Ahah!' and no cathartic release (as sometimes happens), yet I felt my residual restlessness assuaged. I felt 'more myself', 'more together', and 'back in my body' (grounded, centred, balanced).

On this occasion, you may have noted, I attended to dreams and also to changing body sensations and no startling insight arose. For many therapists, especially those from a psychodynamic orientation, this might appear unsatisfactory. It might have seemed so for me too. But on this occasion I felt satisfied. Gestalt is 'process-following' as much as (or more than) 'explanation-seeking'. My state shifted spontaneously here as a result of a process running its course or otherwise re-ordering itself. Value is placed less on 'understanding' and more on 'waking up to' what is happening habitually, by way of thinking, defending, avoiding, etc. In other words there is a shift to direct awareness of 'what one is doing', with the realization that other choices are then possible. However achieved, self-realignment is regarded as existentially responsible (or 'response-able' as it is often spelt). Often, of course, this realigning is done in consort with others – my partner, or close friends, or maybe a shiatsu practitioner. But the responsibility is still mine to initiate or make happen what I need and require for my own well-being, and the capacity to affect others by what I do.

This morning I began by feeling restless. Gestalt psychotherapy's 'paradoxical theory of change' (Beisser, 1970) suggests that changes come about more from fully accepting one's state of being than attempting to fight it and alter it by deliberate means. The process calls for entering more deeply into the 'unwanted' experience, in order to investigate it more inquisitively and also to give space for the possible arising of a spontaneous re-configuring – the destruction of a fixed gestalt, the birth of something new. This almost alchemical process, in which states of being alter often simply as a result of concentrated, non-judgemental attention paid to them, is one of the most crucial insights that gestaltists practise and teach.

As part of sustaining my own sense of well-being, I find remembering the process just described is invaluable in recovering from anxiety or confusion when they arise. For a re-alignment to come about, one needs to 'stand out of the way', shelving one's urgency, and be prepared to tolerate an unstructured moment, a little void of unknowing, into which, taking a deep breath, one heads. 'Trust the process' (if it is allowed to run its course) has become a personal as well as a professional motto.

Engaging with one's state of being in this way is both phenomenological and experimental. Intrinsic as it is to the 'teaching' inherent in gestalt therapy, such attention to departures from wholeness is also akin to meditation practice. Gestalt has strong roots in the wisdom traditions of the Far East, Taoism and Buddhism in particular, so the overlap is not surprising.

6

The festive season is under way. We have risen late, after one of the best dinner parties we have been to in years. Gestalt therapy's attention to 'organismic self-regulation' becomes acutely relevant at times of slight hangovers, as my partner and I gently pick over various possibilities for what to eat and drink for late breakfast. Many possibilities are vetoed at once. Some (like bacon and eggs) are inconceivable today. I settle for an apple and a cup of tea, she for a small plate of cereal and a mug of hot water.

Taking into account the individuality of needs is something that makes a profound impact on those pursuing gestalt practice. The differentiation between people, along with the emphasis on self-regulation, both of which are encouraged and allowed for, is very 'permission-giving'. However, there is ever more recognition that co-regulation is of equal, or even greater, significance, given that our lives are not lived in isolation but always in relation.

How I live gestalt in my personal relationships is a chapter-length topic in itself. In the early days of gestalt, when the individualistic bias of Freudian psychoanalysis (remember that our founders were originally analysts) was still showing at the edges, the 'field' paradigm (emphasizing continuous and inevitable connection between people) was not well developed. Gestalt therapy even became notorious for its 'I do my thing and you do your thing' 1960s-style self-indulgence. In the last twenty years, however, there has been a pronounced swing away from all this toward a more dialogic, relational view of inter-dependent human functioning (e.g. Wheeler, 1991).

During my training, before this change took place, I took on certain guiding values and I feel they have stood me well as principles in my relating to others, even though the inter-subjective and relational language of today is far more sophisticated. They include the following:

- be authentic – say what you mean and mean what you say;
- use 'I' rather than 'one' or 'you' when you actually mean I;
- express differences and work with resentments, instead of harbouring them and papering them over;
- look people in the eye; recognize that one's perceptions of others are largely projective – personal constructions rather than recordings of 'objective reality';
- express appreciations and take risks of heightened intimacy;
- open eyes and ears when taking in another person's reality, give them space, and set aside assumptions;
- recognize the other as a fellow person, a 'Thou' rather than an 'It', and never as simply a label, diagnostic category, or type.

These are all things I still remember. I regret the times I forget, and feel diminished when I become aware of 'missing' another being or of not being present in the moment with them.

Early gestalt therapy focused on 'contact episodes' and was brilliant in its capturing of how moments of full engagement between people come about, and how people learn from them. Last night's party (a fiftieth birthday of one of my longest-known friends) was full of brief encounters, a lot of them significant and energized. They left me (and others, I imagine) feeling touched and satisfied.

Yet life is more than high moments. The more evolved gestalt therapy of the last twenty years has focused more on supporting the ongoing features of relating, including the enduring frameworks that enable relationships to flourish. Connectedness has rhythms and phases; boundaries need to be held; long-term agendas and consequences need to be taken into account. A short-term contact 'high' may be destructive, as well as creative, in the development of someone's whole life. Increasingly, I recognize how stability, continuity, predictability – all challenging for me personally in the past – are necessary in building communities, families and couple relationships. (I have changed, and gestalt therapy has changed too.)

The rebalancing of the early bias has been of critical import. Yet it is to rebalance, not to jettison, the emphasis on intense and truthful contact-making. I am obviously somewhat of a junkie in this regard. I often persist in treating impersonal bureaucrats as 'real people' in the face of their resistance; and I talk to strangers more than most Britons do. I see it as part of my politics of everyday life; to humanize and enliven human settings, and to challenge depersonalizing tendencies.

7

As I continue to reflect, now some time later, on the way I 'live gestalt', the question arises as to what I would have been like had I *not* encountered this body of theory and practice. A short detour is necessary to come to this salient question from the editors.

There is a sensible idea that we are attracted to our specialities according to our basic character and temperament. I remember my first encounter with gestalt therapy. I attended an introductory workshop with mild curiosity, not taking it at all seriously. This rapidly changed. By the end of the three-day event, I knew I had found an approach that made sense to me: I felt I had 'come home'. What was it that spoke to me so profoundly?

In advance, I had no idea what gestalt therapy was, let alone that it was an extraordinary synthesis of many different schools, writers and traditions (including Freud, Reich, Rank, Sullivan, Moreno, Kohler, Friedlander, Lao Tsu, Korzybski, Goldstein, Lewin, Smuts, Dewey, Heraclitus, Suzuki); nor, of course, was I aware that my life and career were about to be up-ended. I had previous experience of academic psychology and of psychoanalytic thinking, and regarded both as 'foreign' to my experience of living. Before gestalt I had been most impacted by the psychological writings of William James: his confident clarity and lack of obfuscation. I felt a strong sense of resonance between James' interest in experience itself, the essence of the gestalt approach as first presented to me, and my own private outlook on life.

Perhaps what most appealed was the central invitation to acknowledge and enter into one's actual experience at the time of its arising, inviting me into levels of authenticity in relationship which I had never encountered hitherto, in any other life context. (Years later, after discovering a major family secret, I realized that gestalt's 'risky truth-telling' aspect was a potent attractor.) Coming into awareness of the present and staying in dialogue with another individual, especially if the other is also attempting to access their personal truth as it arises, is still one of the most usable additions to ordinary life: at least it is for me, and I know it to be so also for others. Once the discipline of staying with one's actual present experience is learned and practised jointly, interpersonal differences and tensions can be rapidly addressed, and more often than not they resolve into greater connectedness and mutual understanding. It is not surprising: after all, most misunderstandings arise from poor listening, projecting, having fantasies about the other, and a variety of ways of dissembling. The opposites serve as powerful antidotes.

The hardest developmental hurdle for me, confronted by the directness and immediacy of the gestalt approach, was to discover my capacity to be fully 'in' my somatic experience, to be wordless, and to trust the spectrum of human feeling reactions that are available if one tunes in to them. I had been desensitized, an intellectualizer for sure, and someone who found non-verbal experiences with others to be uncomfortable. So one answer to the question about 'How would I be without gestalt?' is that I imagine I would probably have still been trying to live as a thinker and analyser first, seeking health and well-being primarily through conceptual understanding, reflection, reading, introspective journal writing, and talking to others. The idea of some unmediated process – stopping, self-attending, entering into the somatic felt sense, and discovering what needed to be expressed – would likely still not have been in my repertoire, any more than would have been the present-centred dialoguing I mentioned in the previous paragraph.

And then, the editors searchingly ask as well, what does *not* fit? Where has gestalt seemed insufficient, or where have I had to look elsewhere for sources of insight and wisdom? Much has been stimulated by living the gestalt discipline but, yes, there are some areas where I personally have felt at odds with the approach, and with the mainstream of the tradition. I am depressed at times by the intellectual laziness and antipathy to ideas that almost killed off the gestalt approach in the 1970s. It has been partly redressed in recent years, though (alas) it is still sometimes evident within the shared professional culture. The gestalt tradition represents a synthesis of some of the most exciting intellectual movements of our epoch. Yet too few gestaltists seem to recognize the barely excavated diamond mine that lies beneath the land on which they have built.

For my taste, there is also too little attention to the arts, though here certainly one does find exceptions (e.g. Zinker, 1977). Overall, the professional culture does not rise up enthusiastically to support a serious engagement with creative artists. The fact is that poets and composers, painters and actors are all absorbed in giving expression to something which comes out of their whole being, drawing on the right as well as left brain, and this parallels the gestalt therapy process itself. Rarely is this depth of similarity acknowledged among the gestalt professional community.

Finally, while many younger gestaltists have moved towards connecting gestalt ways with spiritual disciplines of one kind or another, the original imprint was decidedly secular. Among the founders, there was suspicion of anything smacking of organized religion. While connections have been made, notably with Zen Buddhism, gestalt practice has not embraced, in any serious sense, the notion of service to the needs of the greater whole, despite the fact that its unified field perspective underlines the total interdependence of all beings. There is change afoot here, within the gestalt community, but it has been late in coming.

8

I am now writing away from home, while running a residential group for those with considerable gestalt experience. It is early in the morning and I am propped up in bed, a pad of paper on my knees, and reflecting again on the editors' questions. Not surprisingly, what arises for me this morning has to do with the life of the group I am involved with at the moment.

I set up the group for those who have already had extensive training and personal therapy and who were 'interested in continuing to work with gestalt as a basis for exploring and managing their lives long-term'. Interest was considerable, and the group came into being. I mention this because there are parallels between what I am offering to the group and what I could say I am seeking to offer to myself. Thus, applying gestalt principles and methods to 'explore and manage my life' is an apt description for what I do too.

It is important to realize, from a gestalt point of view, that personal therapy is not regarded as a once-in-a-lifetime matter: further integrations are always possible, and indeed desirable and necessary if we are to continue to evolve. As Sir Isaiah Berlin once pointed out, 'the past is unpredictable', with the past always subject to re-consideration in the light of the present. Aspects of the past arise in present consciousness all the time. I find the whole of my life story and current sense of self are continuously needing updating. Occasional informal therapy with a peer, as well as self-therapy, is required to explore and manage my life, to continue the never-ending integration.

The group I am running here is a meeting place of sixteen intersecting lives (seventeen with mine). Together they are full of plans and prospects, the doings of relatives, new career directions, fluctuations in health status, and changing states of relationships. Circumstances change, fate intervenes, eras end or begin. The topography of personal landscapes is constantly re-shaped, calling for what in gestalt we call 'creative adjustment' (Perls *et al.*, 1951), a more active-sounding process of finding solutions to life's current challenges than is implied in, say, the word 'adaptation'.

Creative adjustment means we encounter newly arising life-moments with fresh thought, innovations in behaviour, courage to cast off into the unknown. No wonder it is something of an ideal and that all of us are inclined to back off from it, favouring 'conservative adjustment' instead. Clinging to the familiar and habitual, we can regress, or fall into old holes, or act out in oft-repeated ways, even if it is damaging to ourselves and others. For me, self-therapy (at least) is called for at times. The fact that I have worked through a huge number of past traumas and developmental issues in therapy does not mean that there is complete immunity from revisiting them, at least partially. Let alone am I proofed against new traumas of a type unmet before? Sometimes, too, an old 'wound' that escaped notice hitherto, is triggered by some contemporary event. For instance, I recently found surprising distress arising in remembering my time in Cambridge as a postgraduate: it arose for me after working therapeutically with a recent Oxford postgraduate who had encountered problems similar to my own.

Most difficulties with creative adjustment occur when major life changes are called for. A crisis is obviously a time to learn most. Yet learning new patterns of being and acting at a time of stress requires real willingness to allow some sense of personal deconstruction. And for this, supportive conditions are necessary. It is the same whether I am working with someone in a group, or with myself in self-therapy: sufficient support for the enterprise is always required if changes are to come about. For myself, I have found that issues of support – the inner strength which I can muster, the back-up I can access and my readiness to call on it, the practical steps of grounding myself, etc. that I remember and utilize – are always significant matters for me (and for others in my life). Recognizing the exact requirements for support calls for great precision.

9

After this rapid tour of how gestalt has infiltrated my life, almost every corner of it, what remains to be said about what I have learned and applied in my life?

First is that what I have described represents a commitment to an examined life. However, that does not mean massive introspection and analysis, or (I hope) self-obsessed egotism. It is more a process of adopting what is described sometimes as the 'witness' position. It involves just noticing, self-forgivingly, what I experience, how I avoid change, what I do to 'protect myself', how I am narcissistic, the ways in which I am choosing actually to live my days. If there is anything that I should like to see gestalt therapy taking on more fully, it is the importance of 'profound self-acceptance'. It parallels teachings from wisdom traditions; it is a natural extension of the paradoxical theory of change; and it represents an existential stance that is light and airy.

Second, in relation to 'embodying the theory', I have always wanted to 'live the approach'. I felt this from Day One of my exposure to gestalt. Then my learning curve was perpendicular, now it is more gradual. Yet there is always more to learn, or to relearn when forgotten. In a line of Rumi's, 'Life is ever pouring in afresh' and life is the ultimate teacher. So intertwined is my gestalt understanding with personal living that as life pours in afresh, so are there consequences in how I work as a psychotherapist. The more I can integrate new life material, the more available I become to clients and trainees.

Last, I can reflect on the future. Holism, as I have said, is central in gestalt philosophy, and many new movements help to sustain this in the world at large. It is not surprising that quite a few gestaltists (including myself) reveal themselves to be organic gardeners, supporters of environmental causes and advocates of complementary medicine. In all of these, holistic outlooks hold sway and are everywhere on the rise.

The gestalt philosopher *par excellence* is Maurice Merleau-

Ponty (alas, barely recognized by the gestalt community). Difficult as he is to read and comprehend, his attempt is always to bring to life the entirety and indivisibility of human living as experienced by a subject. It is the antithesis of the objectifying tendency, the 'it' world, and the so-called 'commonsense' view of reality as being 'out there' with ourselves as separate from it. From a Merleau-Ponty standpoint, and from a postmodernist perspective, as well as from a gestalt one, I am utterly 'intervolved' with the world, creating myself within it, moment by moment. We are pursuing 'a perpetual enterprise of taking our bearings on the constellations of the world' (Merleau-Ponty, 1962). Moreover, Merleau-Ponty emphasizes, being is 'through the intermediary of the body'. The body is the 'vehicle of our being in the world'. Here we find the holistic vision writ large: as living beings we are utterly un-separate from our society, family, culture and relationships, as well as the physical world in which we find ourselves.

In short, the flow of life – to me, through me, out of me – constitutes my being. Self is created moment by moment within a field in flux. Images identifying 'self' as some kind of centralized stable entity; or views of an objective world that is 'out there', durable and separate; or suggestions that life patterns have been effectively 'determined' by past causal influences, all belong to an epistemology that is inimical to gestalt philosophy. However, fully to embrace the implications of the new cosmology (post quantum theory, post chaos theory, etc.) so that it becomes central to the way I live, requires much exploring. It may begin with play and lightness of heart. As I write these words I am conscious that this account veers towards the over-cerebral, despite my beginning to have found another way.

Anyway, it is time to stop. The day is sunny, not unlike the day when I began writing. As I settle the final sentences into shape, I feel aware of wanting to move. Another walk by the river is called for.

References

Beisser, A. (1970) 'The paradoxical theory of change', in J. Fagan and E. L. Shepherd (eds) *Gestalt Therapy Now*. Palo Alto: Science and Behavior Books.

Gendlin, E. (1981) *Focusing*. New York: Bantam Books.

Merleau-Ponty, M. (1962) *Phenomenology of Perception*. London: Routledge and Kegan Paul.

Parlett, M. and Hemming, J. (1996a) 'Gestalt therapy', in W. Dryden (ed.) *Handbook of Individual Therapy*. London: Sage.

Parlett, M. and Hemming, J. (1996b) 'Developments in gestalt therapy', in W. Dryden (ed.) *Developments in Psychotherapy: Historical Perspectives*. London: Sage.

Perls, F. S., Hefferline, R. and Goodman, P. (1951/1994) *Gestalt Therapy: Excitement and Growth in the Human Personality*. Highland, New York: The Gestalt Journal Press.

Perls, L. (1992) *Living at the Boundary*. Highland, New York: The Gestalt Journal Press.

Resnick, R. and Parlett, M. (1995) 'Gestalt therapy: principles, prisms and perspectives' (interview). *British Gestalt Journal*, 4(1), 3–13.

Wheeler, G. (1991) *Gestalt Reconsidered*. New York: Gardner Press.

Yontef, G. (1993) *Awareness Dialogue and Process*. Highland, New York: The Gestalt Journal Press.

Zinker, J. (1977) *Creative Process in Gestalt Therapy*. New York: Brunner/Mazel.

5 | An Infant Personal Construct Theorist (Personal Construct Psychotherapy)

Dorothy Rowe

JOHN MAYNARD KEYNES once remarked that it is ideas which rule the world. Indeed they do, and it is ideas which determine what we as individuals do. Genes may predispose, but it is the ideas which we hold which dispose. Some of these ideas are changeable or fleeting, but other ideas are central to every decision we make and, over our lifetime, change very little.

Some of the ideas which are central to our being we acquire in our earliest years, and the course of our life is greatly influenced by the development and elaboration of these ideas. Much, even most, of our endeavours are concerned with maintaining these ideas and with trying to prove their validity. Our choice of profession, the area in which we choose to research, and the particular theory we espouse are usually, if not always, closely linked to these early but central ideas. Unfortunately my evidence for these last three statements is anecdotal and limited, but I have seen this persistence of ideas acquired early in life in the lives of people whom I have known for many years, in my own life, and in certain biographies which I have read. When I was a student at Sydney University in the 1960s my psychology lecturer Jack Lyle used to sum up this phenomenon with 'the older we get the more like ourselves we become'.

Evidence for the establishment and persistence of ideas is limited because throughout the history of psychology most psychologists failed to see that we are in essence meaning-creating people, and that the creation of meaning and its use should be the subject matter of psychology. We live in meaning like a fish lives in water. The only way we can leave our individual world of meaning is to die. However, to study meaning is to study subjectivity, and, according to these psychologists, subjectivity was bad because it was not scientific. They did not say, though they must have known, that subjectivity is dangerous, because an examination of what we think and feel soon reveals that our lives are not what we want them to be and the world is not what we thought it was. Objectivity promises security, while subjectivity constantly reveals that we each have our own way of seeing things and that our understanding of what actually exists depends on the different individual perceptions of those who are describing what exists.

Autobiographies rarely reveal the acquisition of early and persistent ideas. Until Edward Gosse wrote *Father and Son* in 1907, where he lovingly but truthfully described his father Philip Gosse and the effect this strong-willed, committed Christian had on him as a child, autobiographies were required to say nothing about childhood except that all childhoods were perfect and all parents paragons of virtue. *Father and Son* caused a scandal, but even today, after a century of psychotherapy, most autobiographies skim lightly over childhood and do not explore how the writer came to see himself and his world in his own individual way. To do so would show the imperfections of parents and shatter the myth that childhood is always happy.

Psychotherapists have always been little interested in ideas which do not change, particularly when these ideas appear not to be implicated in the client's distress. We know that when clients change their ideas about their intrinsic wickedness and unacceptability to ideas about their intrinsic goodness and acceptability, profound and beneficial changes follow. I have seen such changes in erstwhile clients with whom I have kept in contact for many years. One such woman wrote to me last Christmas. When we first met twenty years ago she lived a life circumscribed by fear and depression, moving only between her home and work. A visit to my office was a terrifying journey fraught with dangers. In her Christmas letter she casually mentioned, as part of an anecdote, that she had been on holiday in Thailand. Yet certain of her ideas have not changed: her pride in doing her work to the highest standard, her delight in seeing off the men in a game of pool. These are not trivial ideas but central to her maintenance of herself as a person.

Some people would say they have changed their central ideas, but in fact all they have done is to change the garments in which these ideas are dressed. To change from being a Presbyterian to being a Muslim might seem to be a profound change both theologically and socially, but Calvinism and Islam have much in common, not least in the absoluteness of their beliefs and the belief that the holder of the belief is right and everyone else is wrong. Some people may believe that they have abandoned their religious beliefs, only to find that in depression they feel the intense shame and guilt of being possessed of original sin and they await in terror the vengeance of their God. Some people change their beliefs as part of their teenage rebellion, but their action is centred upon the rebellion and not upon working out a totally different set of beliefs. Instead, the teenage rebel, having been taught his parents' beliefs, chooses the exact opposite of these and, since every idea contains its opposite, the new beliefs contain the old. As the years pass the teenage rebel finds it very easy to slip back into the ideas he originally held.

Melvyn Bragg, writer and broadcaster, was such a rebel. He now speaks with scorn of his student self, so unaware of the ineffable mysteries of the Christian religion (Bragg, 1998). In his account of his childhood, Melvyn Bragg described a family and a village life where the range of ideas presented to him was not wide. He attended church and sang in the choir, and was happy doing this. My childhood was very different. I was born into a family which immediately presented me with contrasting ways of interpreting the world. It was not a happy family and for me it was a dangerous family. Perhaps with that precocious intelligence developed by an infant born to a mother who cannot mother which Alice Miller described in *The Drama of the Gifted Child* (1983), I learnt that I had to be keenly aware of what was going on around me if I were to survive both physically and as a person. In effect, I had a choice of becoming an infant personal construct psychologist, going mad, or dying. In the first four or five years of my life I created at least four ideas which became central to my existence and, later, central to the psychological theory which I developed. These ideas were:

- Each of us has our own way of seeing things.
- Absolute beliefs and absolute power are always dangerous and must be resisted.
- I must always be sceptical. All ideas and beliefs must be tested against what is actually happening.
- The natural world is beautiful and can be relied upon to sustain and comfort, but it must be seen as it is and not as I might wish it to be.

Stated like this, these ideas seem to have a maturity and complexity far beyond the understanding of a small child. Yet I did form them. I could not have articulated these ideas, but, in a form more of images and feelings rather than words, they gave a structure to my experience, they were constantly reinforced by my experience, and they kept me safe.

I now realize that, in one respect at least, I was extremely lucky to have the parents that I did. Unfortunate indeed is the child who is born to parents who present a consistent view of the world. The poor child may fail to see that such consistency does not really represent the idiosyncratic perceptions of each parent but is a conspiracy by the parents to force the child into obedience and conformity to what the parents want. The child is likely to grow up believing that there is one right way of seeing things and that whenever his views differ from those in authority he is at fault. This has been the fate of many of our clients. Of course my parents would have liked me to be obedient and to conform, but the diversity of their views often allowed me to escape their demands that I be a good child.

Every day I was presented with evidence that each of us has our own way of seeing things. My mother was a pessimist. The universe failed to live up to her expectations, and this disgusted and angered her enormously. She always expected the worst. There was no event of good fortune from which she could not predict doom and disaster. My father was an optimist. For him the universe was a constant source of interest, delight and hope. Daily my parents gave me a lesson in alternative construing, with my mother interpreting some event as wicked and disastrous, and my father saying to her, 'Can't you look on the bright side?' Moreover, my father loved people and was a friend to everyone he met. My mother hated strangers, and a stranger was anyone who was not immediate family. Since I could see that usually each of my parents had a point, I learnt that people are always a mixture of the good and the bad. For me all heroes have clay feet.

In contrast to my parents, my sister, six years older than me, operated on a simple but effective construct, 'of use to me/of no use to me'. Events and people who were designated 'of no use to me' ceased, in her eyes, to exist. On occasions I was deemed to be 'of use to me' and she would use me, but most of the time I did not exist. Whenever she stumbled across me (we shared a bedroom) she was greatly irritated. In her adult life my sister wrote a brief history of our family for a book about Irish families in Australia and in another history of life in Australia she contributed a family story. In neither of these accounts do I feature, neither in the list of children my parents had nor in the story of which I was one of the participants. As an adult I can laugh about being written out of history, but in my childhood similar acts of annihilation by my sister and my mother I found utterly terrifying. I struggled to understand why the terror of being annihilated as a person was far greater than the terror of death, but out of these struggles and out of the conversations with people who were describing similar experiences I came to see how primary is our need to maintain ourselves as a person.

So here were three points of view, to which I added a fourth. Thus I knew that everything could be seen in a multitude of ways, and as a result, whenever at home or school or church I was presented with an absolute truth, I could see it only as part of a person's point of view and not as a truth which existed eternally outside time and space. This way of thinking was reinforced by my political and religious education.

My father was a socialist, and in those days socialism had the connotations of nobility and virtue. I had been born in the midst of the Great Depression when many Australians lost their jobs and homes and many were close to starvation. As a small child I knew that the devil had a name and it was Montague Norman, the Governor of the Bank of England, whose policies created such misery. I was 5 when the Spanish Civil War broke out. I learned that evil had a name, and it was fascism. I learned that we ignore politics at our peril, and that politics are not separate from us but part of our daily life. When I went to university, how I despised those psychologists who had divided psychology into social and individual. How could they be so stupid?

I asked myself this question again and again during the years of the Thatcher Government when I was in charge of the Lincolnshire Department of Clinical Psychology. There we saw many depressed former steelworkers, ignorant of politics and economics, who blamed themselves for the closure of the British Steel factories in Scunthorpe. We also saw a new phenomenon: post-natal depression in men who were now unemployed and staying at home to mind their small children while their wives obtained work as secretaries and shop assistants. Surely this phenomenon could not be explained solely in terms of hormones in the way that post-natal depression in women was traditionally explained?

My religious education showed me that there are as many religious beliefs as there are people to hold them. My mother insisted that I attend the Presbyterian church and Sunday

School, but she did not go to church, partly because she was frightened to go among strangers and partly because she was not going to have a man tell her what to do. My father did not attend church because he had no religious beliefs and despised the hypocrisy of many of the Christians he had met during the First World War and in business. Often in the evenings after dinner he would read to us. One of his favourite books was *Lectures and Essays* by R. G. Ingersoll. Ingersoll was an American lawyer, born in 1833, and one of the great American orators. His essay 'The Gods' begins:

> An honest god is the noblest work of man. Each nation has created a god, and the god has always resembled his creators. He hated and loved what they hated and loved, and he was invariably found on the side of those in power. Each god was intensely patriotic, and detested all nations but his own. All these gods demanded praise, flattery and worship. (Ingersoll, 1945)

In defence against the utter boredom of the church services I would listen to the minister preaching and would read my hymnbook and catechism and understand what Ingersoll had said.

My religious education increased my scepticism but it also enabled me to see that the meaning we give to the nature of death and the purpose of life is not tangential to our life but central to it. Many years later this became the theme of my second book, *The Construction of Life and Death*, which my present publishers, who always want a cheery title, now call *The Courage to Live*.

Some years ago I was invited to take part in a programme in a BBC Radio 4 series called *Devout Sceptics*. The unstated aim of this series was to show that all of those interviewed by the journalist Bel Mooney would, through skilled questioning, finally reveal that actually, after all, they did hold religious beliefs. I failed to perform as predicted, and I was greatly surprised that my interview was broadcast. I suspect that my statement that I am very fond of trees was construed as some kind of arboreal religion. During the actual interview Bel Mooney could not accept that I had never had a belief in God, and she came back time and time again to press me on this issue. Afterwards this set me wondering how a belief in someone who is not physically present can take root. I contrasted my belief in the existence, albeit terminated, of my father's father with my lack of belief in the existence of God. My father was a great story-teller. When I was little I would ask him for stories about when he was a boy. Invariably his story would involve his father, who was a very fine man by my father's account. He had been killed in a mining disaster when my father was 16, but to me he was a very real person. In contrast, neither of my parents talked about God as if He existed. Indeed they never mentioned God at all. Only in extreme situations might they exclaim, 'Oh, God!' I imagine that in homes where God is talked about as an active participant in the family's life, where prayers are said and where there are pictures and altars and other mementoes, in the young child's mind the concept 'God' is likely to come to represent a real, though invisible, person, and that representation persists for the rest of the child's life. God becomes an internal object for that person, just as my father's father is one of the group of people I carry within me.

For me to say that I have or had a belief in the existence of God would be to deny my own truth. I now know that lying to ourselves is perhaps the most dangerous thing we can do, but when I was a child I learnt that for my own safety I should not take anything on trust, I should be certain about what I thought and felt, and that I must see the world as it is and not through a veil of needs and wishes. Nowadays, if I am writing about how a small child develops his understanding of himself and the world around him, I will talk about how important it is that parents reinforce the child's meanings by accepting them, and offer modifications to improve their validity in a gentle, encouraging manner, and not use criticism, condemnation and humiliation to force the child to think differently. My father used these gentle methods with me, but his work took him away from home. I spent most of my time with my mother and sister. My mother believed that praise inevitably 'spoilt' a child. Her criticisms of me were endless, and she set an example which my sister followed whenever she stumbled across me. I feared being shamed and humiliated, so I learned to keep my thoughts to myself.

However, being told that I was wrong, stupid, silly, frequently led me to doubt my perceptions, and so I developed habits of checking my ideas against reality and of asking myself whether I was pretending to feel something which I did not feel. What was most devastating to me was my mother's habit of telling me I was lying whenever I said something which did not fit with the way she wanted to see the world. My sister did the same. These assaults on my perceptions had a very profound effect on me, and, in my teens and early twenties, on the occasions when I lost confidence in myself, I came close to losing my grip on reality. Years later, in conversations with people diagnosed as schizophrenic, I heard stories where each of these people, in childhood, had had the meanings they had created denied and rejected. In one family I knew, the young son would see that his mother was upset and crying after she had been verbally abused by her husband. He would go to comfort her, but she would insist that she was happy, that her husband was not angry, and that everything was perfect. Some years later, when the lad had become psychotic, the mother told me that she thought she had been protecting her son by pretending that nothing was amiss. However, her lies and the lies the philandering father told undermined the boy's confidence in his own perceptions. If over the past century psychiatrists had sought to understand what goes on in families and how parental behaviour affects the development of the child instead of devoting themselves to trying to find mythical pink spots or defects in brain structure or mental illness genes, all considered causative of schizophrenia, our understanding and care of those who become psychotic would be far in advance of the knowledge and care that we have today.

As small children we need to develop confidence in the meanings we create, and we need to learn how to distinguish those meanings which are a fairly good representation of what is actually going on from those meanings we call fantasy. We need, too, to understand where fantasy is appropriate and where it is not. Fantasy can be very useful in restoring our equilibrium after some personal failure ('This is what I would have said if I had thought of it at the time'), planning our future ('If I take that job then . . .'), and providing a distraction when we need to stop worrying in order to rest ('Once upon a time . . .'). However, our theories about other people and what is actually going on are fantasies until we test them against reality. Often we prefer to hang on to a fantasy, even though it makes us miserable, rather than risk finding out what is really happening. Our fantasy makes us feel important and reality might show that we are not. Those people who are given the now fashionable diagnosis of social phobia often choose to continue in their misery because they prefer their fantasy that everybody is looking at them and despising them to the reality that no one is interested in them at all. When no one acknowledges our existence we can come close to annihilation.

Without fantasy children would not survive childhood. Fantasy compensates them for disappointment and gives them encouragement and hope. However, the more a child is disappointed and the more a child feels discouraged and hopeless, the more the child has to rely on fantasy to survive and the less the fantasies relate to the real world and real possibilities. One of the sad things that happens to many children is that they lose the curiosity and delight in the world around them with which they were born. Perhaps they have been punished all too often for their curiosity and delight; perhaps they have come to feel such disgust with themselves that this disgust spills out and poisons all that is around them. Along with these experiences can come a profound distrust of other people who they see either as too worthy and virtuous to be close to or as hiding their wickedness under a veneer of goodness. Children who come to see the world and other people in this way have to create fantasies which do not relate to this world and to ordinary people. They have to fantasize special, magical people and places outside time and space. They cannot derive comfort and hope from the real world and from real people but have to rely on their fantasies which they call their religious or spiritual or magical beliefs. They do not believe that life can be satisfying and happy when it is lived in terms of the real world and real people. They try to find happiness in imaginary worlds, and they fear the loss of their beliefs because then life would become utterly hopeless. There are many such people. When I review my life I can wonder why I did not join their number. The answer I arrive at is very simple: my mother was lazy and my father liked people.

My mother did not like leaving the safety of her home and she was careless of my physical safety. I could wander in the bush or play at the beach as I wished. It was just my good fortune that I was never lost in the bush, or kidnapped, or bitten by a poisonous snake or eaten by a shark. It was also my good fortune that I always had a place of refuge and delight. The trees in the bush and the vast ocean seemed to me to provide the reassurance and encouragement which the adults in my life failed to supply.

I now live in London where, at the front of my flat, I look into the trees of Highbury Fields, and in the garden at the back I have grown a fine array of trees, shrubs and flowers. Summer and winter, there is always something beautiful to rest my eyes upon. Moreover, the garden always gives me something new to think about. This spring my wattle tree (mimosa), now five years old and grown ten feet tall, bloomed for the first time, covering itself with soft yellow balls of blossoms.

It was her fear of other people which kept my mother at home, but she would not acknowledge this fear and instead turned it into a disgust and rejection of the human race. As a result she lived what I saw as an extremely boring and limited life. I refused to do the same. Though a number of people have hurt and betrayed me, I have always seen the wisdom of my father's view that most people are basically good and worth getting to know. The belief that the real world and other people can be the source of contentment and happiness has enabled me to work with my clients in a framework of encouragement and hope, despite the fact that many of them have berated me for being so foolishly optimistic. It gives me great pleasure now to see that many of my erstwhile clients have worked out for themselves that ordinary life can bring immense contentment and satisfaction.

By the time I went to university I was convinced that it was tremendously important to discover what actually went on in the world. This included finding out how other people saw themselves and their world. Alas, this view had little relevance to the kind of psychology I encountered at the Sydney University in 1948. It was about large, unwieldy theories of learning and the miraculous discovery that people learned meaningful sentences more quickly than they learned strings of nonsense syllables. When I graduated I forsook psychology and did not return to it until 1961 when I trained as an educational psychologist and later did my Diploma of Clinical Psychology at Sydney University. While training as an educational psychologist I was given a piece of advice which I subsequently found to be infallible. It was, 'the presenting problem is never the real problem'. Listen to your clients and listen for the reasons behind the reasons.

The Diploma of Clinical Psychology course was largely psychoanalytical but taught in terms of how we create meaning and the different kinds of meaning we can create. Not for a minute did I consider that there were real entities of an id, an ego and super-ego lodged inside me, any more than I considered that also lodged in me were factors, traits or lumps of intelligence. All of these terms simply related to ideas which might or might not be useful in understanding why we do what we do.

By 1965 my marriage had ended and in 1968 my young son and I went to England where I obtained a National Health Service job in the psychiatric clinic attached to the Department of Psychiatry at Sheffield University. Alec Jenner, now Emeritus Professor, suggested to me that I join his team of researchers who were aiming to find the metabolic basis of mood change. I could study 'psychological aspects of people with regular mood change'. As it turned out, the metabolic basis of mood change was completely elusive, as were the people with regular mood change, but Alec's suggestion did set me on a very interesting path.

In those days all psychological tests were reliable and were not designed to measure change. At a lecture in the Department of Psychology at Sheffield University I heard mention of repertory grids. More importantly, I worked with the psychologist Peter Clarke who was a close friend of Don Bannister. Peter gave me my first encounter with laddering by laddering me. As I reached the top of my ladder my heart was beating furiously, which was a good lesson for me. After this experience I was not likely to see this questioning process as purely a cognitive exercise.

[For those readers unfamiliar with personal construct theory: laddering is a systematic way of asking questions which uncovers the reasons behind the reasons until the ultimate reason, or the top of the person's ladder, is reached. This ultimate reason has to do with how the person experiences his sense of existence. Although this can be expressed in a multitude of ways, these ways fall into two distinct groups: those people who experience their existence in terms of relationships to other people and for whom annihilation is rejection and abandonment, and those people who experience their sense of existence in terms of the development of the individual, of control, achievement and organization, and for whom annihilation is chaos. The first group I call 'People Persons' or extraverts, and the second 'What Have I Achieved Today Persons' or introverts.

Suppose the client indicates, perhaps by emphasis or choice of adjectives, that keeping his home clean and tidy is important to him. I could then ask, 'Why is keeping your home clean and tidy important to you?' Answers to this question go in one of two directions. The first is when the person replies with, 'A clean and tidy house is a welcoming house. And what would people think of me if the place was dirty?'

'Why is it important to you that your home be welcoming?'

'I want my friends to visit me of course.'

'Why is it important to you that your friends visit you?'

'That's what life's about – friends, relationships.' This is the top of the person's ladder.

Another person might answer the question 'Why is keeping your home clean and tidy important to you?' with 'Because chaos makes me nervous. By being organized and in control I'm efficient.'

'Why is it important to you to be efficient?'

'Because that's how I achieve what I want to achieve.'

'Why is it important to you to achieve?'

'Because that's what life's about.' This is the top of the person's ladder.

Of course we all want to have a sense of achievement and enjoy good relationships, but often life forces us to choose, and if we fail to choose what is the most important to us we suffer. I have found that introverts always know what is the most important to them but many extraverts do not, usually because they find it difficult to distinguish what they do from why they do it.]

I went to a summer school run by Don Bannister, Fay Fransella, Miller Mair and Phil Salmon, and felt that at last I had met a group of psychologists who were trying to develop a psychology which related to what human beings actually are: meaning-creating creatures. I cannot say that I had found a theory which I would subsequently espouse. I came to realize that Kellian theory was not the best starting point for developing an understanding of how constructs form the meaning structure which is our person or self, and how we have to develop defences to prevent our meaning structure from being annihilated by events or by attacks made on it by other people, all of which formed the basis of my subsequent work. What I did find was a set of words which formed a useful label and a group of people who were markedly wiser than most of the psychologists I had previously encountered.

Psychologists love abstract nouns and make great use of them even when there is nothing in reality to which they relate. Categorizing their fellows is tremendously important to them. My interactions with psychologists became easier once I had the label of 'personal construct psychologist'. Of course I saw the other personal construct psychologists as wise because they held very much the same views as I did. They knew that it was vitally important to study how people created meaning; they respected the relative truths held by individuals; they were sceptical of absolute truths; they preferred to know what actually went on rather than mislead themselves with elaborate theories; and they believed that we can, by reconstruing, create a life for ourselves which is positive and worthwhile. Moreover, they were devising new methods of research and sharing their discoveries with one another. They had not created a closed order of very special psychotherapists who were privy to some great secret, and where entry to the order was by prolonged and difficult examinations to determine whether the applicant had acquired only those ideas in which the order believed. Instead, as personal construct psychologists we could have our own ideas, pursue our individual lines of enquiry, and discuss, agree or argue as we wished. This meant that personal construct psychology would never become a powerful school of psychotherapy. For an organization to become powerful it has to be authoritarian and claim to be in possession of some absolute truth.

However, I do get a great deal of satisfaction out of knowing that the results of recent neurological studies of brain function seem to give a physiological underpinning to personal construct theory. These studies show that the connections which are created in an individual's brain between neurones relate directly to that individual's experience. No two brains ever have the same patterns of connections because no two people ever have the same experience. Similarly, no two people ever see themselves and their world in exactly the same way because no two people ever have the same experience. It is by no means certain that neuronal patterns form the physiological substratum of all the meanings we create, but research over the next decade or two should be able to spell out more completely the relationship between neural patterns and personal constructs (see Greenfield, 1995).

Meanwhile I shall continue my study of ideas and be glad that my early and central ideas proved to be so fruitful and satisfying.

References and further reading

Bragg, M. (1998) in BBC Radio 4 Programme *Devout Sceptics*.

Gosse, E. (1907) *Father and Son*. Harmondsworth: Penguin, 1988.

Greenfield, S. (1995) *Journey to the Centers of the Mind*. New York: W. H. Freeman & Co.

Ingersoll, R. G. (1945) *Lectures and Essays*. London: Watts & Co.

Miller, A. (1983) *The Drama of the Gifted Child*. London: Faber & Faber.

Rowe, D. (1982) *The Construction of Life and Death*. Chichester: John Wiley.

Rowe, D. (1991) *The Courage to Live*. London: HarperCollins.

6 The Body I Am: Lived Body and Existential Change (Existential Psychotherapy)

Miles Groth

I HAVE NOT ALWAYS held the view that I now support. When I first realized that I wanted to work with people in some way that would help them toward change, if they wanted to change, I turned to psychoanalysis. My training included a didactic analysis with a classical Freudian analyst three times a week for five years. True to form, I soon found myself looking for the unconscious motivations of the actions and feelings of my family, colleagues, students and friends. I developed a taciturn persona, quietly waiting for the other person to betray his hidden wishes, so that I could understand the 'real' meaning of his overt behaviour. As a result, I lost a few friends, who understandably objected to my 'wild' interpretations of their hidden motives.

I must admit, however, that I felt more at home with myself as a result of the psychoanalytic explorations and excavations to which I submitted myself. Psychoanalytic investigation yielded revelations about many (though certainly not all) of the peculiarities of my personality. At the same time, however, I felt a fresh veneer of unhappiness covering what I had uncovered. This was who I had become, I thought, and I could live with it. I was the result of forces that had formed me during early childhood, and that was that. The only difference, as a result of analysis, was that I accepted who I was.

I soon realized, however, that the remainder of discontent, even sadness, I now felt resulted from seeing my life as a *fait accompli*. There was a sobering negativity about the judgement that nothing could be done to change the basic contours of my life. At that point, I seriously began to challenge the assumptions of the psychoanalytic point of view. I already knew Heidegger quite well. As early as 1982, I had published a paper in the *International Review of Psycho-Analysis* on the notion of interpretation in Freud and Heidegger (Groth, 1982), but I had not fully appreciated the scope of what I said there. Still a card-carrying psychoanalyst at heart, I was not yet prepared to relieve myself of the assumption that who I was could not change and that I could not revise the basic assumptions about my life. Then, at one of those moments of fundamental existential change which I subsequently came to regard as so important, I realized I was no longer the person I had been at the end of my analysis.

Existential change

A concept of existential change has become one of the elements of my theory of practice. People change over from one way of being to another 'in the twinkling of an eye' – *im Augenblick*, as the Germans say. My favourite examples of this include the boy who, for many months, has been growing in stature, undergoing the metamorphosis of puberty. Bits of hair have been showing up at the corners of his mouth, pubic hair has been sprouting, and his voice has been creaking in its descent to a lower register. The boy has noticed all of these physical changes with great interest and often with some apprehension. He is, however, still playing with the toys of his childhood, although he has added some of the paraphernalia of adolescent games to the mix. Physically, he has been maturing, and as we know from physics, biological changes, like all events in nature, occur gradually, seamlessly, and without sudden leaps. But then, one morning, he wakes up (perhaps after having had a wet dream the night before), walks up to the bathroom mirror, into which he has gazed every day of his young life (recently with special interest), and sees that he is no longer a boy. He is a man. This is a moment of existential change. He will never see himself as a boy again. Later that week, he may gather up his small-fry games and toys and put them away in a box in the basement, and never take them seriously as toys again. Perhaps many years later, in middle age, he will come across them, but/these artifacts of another world will seem as foreign to him as the equipment of an aboriginal culture.

Or there is the example of a woman, whose skin has been losing some of its elasticity for several years as she approaches menopause. She, too, examines her face in the mirror every day. Oestrogens are produced erratically now, her metabolism adjusts and readjusts to changing quantities of the hormones, and her body inexorably ages, slowly drying up. Like the changes of puberty, such changes occur slowly. But then, one afternoon, this woman pauses in front of the mirror above the mantelpiece in her living room and, there, facing her, is a different woman. She has changed. She is no longer a young woman. She is past her physical prime. Like the Marschallin in *Der Rosenkavalier*, she sees she is old.

Such existential change is what matters for us: for the young man, who must now understand what has been happening during the months since the onset of his puberty, or for the woman, who must comprehend the inevitable physical decline that her body has endured. In each case, the world of the individual has changed. Existence and world change together. In my own case, I had changed, although it took me some time to see just what had happened. I learned that it is in the nature of some transformations that the individual realizes a change has occurred, but does not know what he has become. Change in existential analysis often happens in this way.

Every culture recognizes changes of this kind and provides rituals to acknowledge them. Rites have been established to mark existential changes of status that affect a person's life in the community. Here I think of the marriage vows ('I do!'), the pronouncements made in legal proceedings ('We find you guilty!'), and the *rites de passage*.

My work as an existential analyst focuses on the singular and unique existential changes that my clients undergo, the remarkable turning points in which an individual is transformed in such a way that, for example, his world has narrowed oppressively or widened to such an extent that it is impossible for him to find his bearings in it. Such changes were masterfully described by Jonathan Swift in *Gulliver's Travels*, in which a puny and helpless Gulliver experiences the macroscopic world of the Brobdingnagians or moves gingerly among the microscopic Lilliputians who loom in ghastly excess in his world (Swift, 1726).

I realized that, at such moments of change, everything changes, not just the balance of structures and libidinal forces in one's psyche. The world changes. Everything is different in it. Here my theoretical guide has been the Dutch phenomenological psychologist, Jan van den Berg, whose theory of metabletics (van den Berg, 1971) inspired an essential part of my own theory. I was thus not *gradually* no-longer-a-psychoanalyst. At a certain point of changeover, I was an existential analyst, regardless of what I had been before. It took me many months to realize what I had become and to understand the consequences of the change.

Such changes are occurring all the time, every day, although we do not readily see them because they are not very dramatic. They are none the less important existentially, however, for being less noticeable. When I finish writing (or revising) this text, I will have changed, perhaps in an important way that it will take me months to comprehend. Having met someone new, I will have changed. This 'future perfect' comprehension of what has happened is a basic feature of our lives.

I am not suggesting that such change is constant: that would place it on the same footing as physical change. I am only saying that existential changes are common in the course of most days. As we learn from Freud, a seemingly trivial event can affect a whole lifetime. I would describe such events as existentially significant, although perhaps affectively under-registered, events which are only weakly (if at all) recollectable.

In my own life, I find that as a consequence of thinking about things in this way, my experience of other people outside of the consulting room is more attuned to the existential changeovers of their lives. As a result, I am more patient with my colleagues and friends, students and family. I am on the lookout for whether things have changed for them. If so, I give them time to work out the consequences of such change, which may take days, weeks, or even months.

On the other hand, I have given up waiting for people to change. Nor do I view my work in existential analysis as geared toward effecting change. However, I am in a good position to see that things have changed in a client's life and I often point this out to him. As already suggested, often enough he does not see that he has changed. Only after some days or even months will he have reckoned with what happened. Unless I am fairly certain about what I think has changed for the person, I withhold comment, yet even if I speak out and am wrong in such cases, no harm has been done. An invitation has been made to verify or disconfirm that things have changed.

My work as a teacher has also been affected by my theory of existential change. The occurrence of insight among students is an important example of such change. Insight cannot be forced: it usually comes out of the blue. Sometimes it comes as the summation of a series of logical steps taken, but just as often it happens on the heels of an intuition or as a result of the work of imagination. I now also see the centrality of insight in my own work. Insight comes, not so much as the result of a concerted effort to reach a new perspective, but quite suddenly, unexpectedly, while listening to a client, reading a passage, writing a sentence, or reflecting.

It is as fruitless to try to force insight in another human being, whether a student or client in therapy, as it is to compel insight in oneself. In either case, I have found that it is best to wait. Perhaps my student's intellectual exercises come to nothing. I take that in my stride, realizing at the same time that it is always valuable to offer students encouragement without expecting anything from them. In psychotherapy, insight occurs as existential change, whether the change is gratifying or disturbing.

My approach to writing has been affected by recognizing that insight is a form of existential change. I never make an outline of what I want to say. Instead, I sit down to write and wait to see what, if anything, will emerge. Sometimes my starting point is a text that I have set out to interpret. Other times, I want to clarify a concept for myself or for an audience. In every case, I wait for the theme of my essay to reveal itself.

Existential change is both active and acceptive. The ultimate change is from life to death. As we know from Heidegger's notion of being-toward-death (Heidegger, 1962), death is the change that cannot be outwitted. No further change can follow the changeover to being dead. Death is therefore the prototype for all existential change, in that existential changes are irreversible. Thus, although it is very unlikely, I might move on to again being a psychoanalyst, but I would not be the same kind of psychoanalyst I was before I became an existential therapist. I cannot return to where I once was existentially. As Thomas Wolfe (1989) wrote: 'You Can't Go Home Again.' Implicit in this view is that the succession of episodes in one's life is not repeatable. My life may circle back to the vicinity of a previous world, but the movement is a widening or narrowing spiral.

The affective component of existential change dominates the experience of such transformation. When things have changed, I find myself living in a different key, attuned differently. Although I am always in a mood, only when things have changed do I notice my mood. Conversely, when I notice my mood, my world has usually changed. When I am attuned differently, I handle things differently. I notice, for example, that I am fumbling with things or that my movements have taken on an especially satisfying rhythm, as though they had been choreographed. Playing the piano, my performance is facile, or clumsy. My handwriting is fluent and regular, or it is hurried and indecipherable. When I speak, my voice rests comfortably in a resonant register, or it is raspy and dissonant. My gait is sure, or I stumble. In the changeover from one to the other of these contrasting indications of how I am in the world, a change in my existence can be inferred.

The existential present

Another element of my existential theory has to do with the experience of time. In recollection, each of us has access to his own past. There is evidence of that past in our bodies, especially their involuntary habits and patterns of movement, including the way we speak, as well as the features our physical bodies bear (wrinkles, scars, our physiognomy, posture and bearing). In imagination, we have access to our future, which we project from out of the possibilities we invent using the materials of our past. Of course, the future is always capable of departures that our past could never have anticipated. But what of my present, the very upsurge of my existence?

It seems to me that we do not have direct access to our present. It is not part of us, like our past, or a realm which may be imagined, like our future. We are always so caught up in making present, that is, our existence, that if we attempt to have this present as an object of reflection, it eludes us. It has already slipped into our past or we are minutes, even years, ahead of ourselves in imaginative anticipation of the future. This holds for all actions, involuntary and voluntary. Thus, if I try to examine my gait as I am walking, I am in for a tumble, or if I try to examine my speech as I am talking, I stutter and experience a kind of motor aphasia. Certainly, I have in mind what I want to articulate, but just what I will have said (unless I am reading from a prepared text or delivering a speech from memory) always remains to be heard.

But does anyone have access to my present? Yes. Others can have direct access to my present. It is for this reason that we need them. They are witnesses to our present. In infancy, the present is initially bestowed on us by a mothering figure, who therefore can be said to confer our existence on us. Subsequently, others continue to validate our existence, in three primary modes: looking at us, speaking to us, and touching us. These are the three basic modes of existential validation, although there are others. All of this points to the inevitability of others in our lives as human beings; in other words, to our essential coexistence (*Mitdasein*, to use Heidegger's term (Heidegger, 1962)) with others.

We must acknowledge the singularity of the mother–child relationship, which is the model for all later relationships in all their ambiguity and ambivalence. For many months, a mother touches her infant without feeling the mutuality of existential validation, sensing that she must first confer on her child his existence, which, soon after psychological birth, can then engage her in mutual validation.

What I *am* is caught up in my past and, in a version of what I am, is projected from out of it into the imagined future – but my present is nothing at all. It *is* not. This is precisely what allows it to be the site of existential change. Compared to the actuality of my past, which provides a range of possibilities for me, my present is the realization of one of those possibilities, which the future receives as real. Existence has its source in this present. Like the present, my existence is nothing at all.

The necessity of others in bestowing our existence on us is shown by the exceptions; for example, feral children such as Victor, the wild boy of Aveyron (Lane, 1979), and perhaps some autistic children. The ongoing importance of others as the witnesses of my present may also be confirmed by considering the unusual personalities of so-called schizophrenics, whose chief symptom is affective and social withdrawal from others. We may understand the retraction of their existence as a consequence of the absence in their lives of the existential witnessing and validation that others provide. Bereft of existence, they have nothing to offer for validation and cannot meet and validate the existence of others. Such individuals show the great vulnerability of the present, i.e. of existence. In general, as people age and become more isolated or when they are socially marginalized and ignored, they too become peculiar, precisely because of the very limited endorsement or validation of their present (hence, of their existence) by others.

Just as I accept my dependence upon others for the ongoing validation of my existence, I recognize my responsibility for their existence. Incidentally, what I have described here is as close to an ethical position based on existential theory as I can identify. As such, it has provided me with a basis for action as a moral agent. With the exception of that extraordinary event of maternal existence-bestowing, existential witnessing is always bilateral and mutual. I cannot validate the existence of another person unless he validates my existence. This is observable in the three primary modes of existential validation mentioned above: the gaze, touching, and speech. (Much of this I owe to John Heron's study of the phenomenology of social encounter (Heron, 1970)). Certainly, I can look at another person without meeting his existence. He may not see me looking at him, or he may avert his gaze. Or I can examine his eyes as objects. If I avert my gaze when the other's look is directed to me, I derail the process of validation. When our gazing is mutual, however, we have witnessed each other's existence.

Similarly, when I merely examine another person's body with my hand, I fail to endorse his existence. Thus the physician's hand investigates my body and the physiotherapist's massage manipulates my flesh. When touching is mutual, however, as in a handshake or an embrace, or in sexual intercourse, it is an act of mutual validation. The limp hand of the schizophrenic lies in my hand like a dead fish. He lets me hold on to it, but bars the witnessing of his existence just as he sabotages the validation of my existence. A person who refuses my embrace lets his body be squeezed but short-circuits the mutual validation of our existence. Finally, there is speech, which is the most remarkable of the three modes of existential validation. I may address someone with my words or give him orders. In doing so, I do not expect a response. By contrast, implies both a listener and his answer. Here we ther's existence. In dialogue, we again and again circle of mutuality that existential validation ..pnes. The necessity of taking turns in speaking to one another masks conversation's mutuality, which is so evident in the gaze and in touch.

As a teacher, I am oriented by the mutuality of conversation between my students and me. As we all know, good teaching, regardless of whatever else may enter into the equation, makes the student feel brighter and more apt. That is its primary goal, as Socrates' erotic maieutics demonstrated in his conversation with young Meno a long time ago (see Plato, 1961). If I catch myself lecturing my students, I realize that in my soliloquizing, I am merely talking at them. I might as well not be there. An image of me on a television screen would do. Much to my horror, I see that this often happens now in American secondary and even post-secondary education.

In the therapeutic setting, as in teaching and everyday talk, I strive to maintain what, following Martin Buber, one might call I–Thou discourse (Buber, 1974). Regardless of what the psychoanalytic theory of therapy may have to say about active listening, the one-sided monologue encouraged in the psychoanalytic setting inevitably fails to allow the mutually validating experiences that effective psychotherapy requires. As a therapist, I must be in the ambit of the other's world. If one of the preconditions of effective psychotherapy is existential validation, the psychoanalytic ideal of a therapeutic blank screen would be undesirable, even if it were attainable.

Dialogue in existential analysis amounts to mutual validation of the existence of both client and analyst. Many individuals whose present is not reflected for them in the ways I have mentioned become our clients in existential psychotherapy. I think it would not be incorrect to say that effective existential analysis is marked by the restoration of the client's present. In the mutuality of therapeutic dialogue, we have also hit upon one of the reasons that doing existential analysis is so satisfying. By contrast, the abstinence required of psychoanalysts is enervating, and I think this may account for the gloominess of so many of my analytic colleagues.

In developing this view, it occurred to me that while other people play the role I have outlined above, so do things, especially the living things that populate nature. Considered together, people and things are places, sites where my world occurs. Things encounter us. We do not happen to stumble across them and make use of them, as the standard instrumental account of our relations with non-human entities has it. Instead, like human beings, things beckon to us and we attend to them. We may quickly turn away from them, or we may linger with them, contemplate them and, in some cases, even make use of them. The traditional Marxian view of the use-nature of things, which has come to dominate modern life, fails to recognize the original encountering *of* things, this 'of' understood in both the objective and subjective genitive senses of the word.

My understanding of the nature of things is due in part, once again, to what I learned from van den Berg, but I find that, without attempting to do so, I have adopted a view that is also congenial with elements of Zen Buddhism. Finally, in my take on our relation to things, there are also elements of Heidegger's notion (adapted from Meister Eckhart) of *Gelassenheit* (Heidegger, 1969), of the acceptive relation to things that does not appropriate them, but rather frees them up and allows them to encounter us. Domination of things by forceful appropriation of them forecloses an appreciation of our acceptive openness to things. As a result, we hold things at a distance, subject them to the examining look, and must then search for ways to re-establish contact with them.

In contrast to the view of the natural sciences, which emphasizes the questioning observer (who is the model of the scientist), I see that things interrogate me. I experience things as inviting a response from me, not as candidates for my dominance and control. Consequently, things can not come to hold me in thrall, which can happen only when they are objects subject to my power. Only then can things come to fascinate me. It may well be that such fascination is the basis for what we incorrectly term the addictions, for it is clear that things hold sway in the addict's world. But fascination with things is possible only when they are regarded as 'suspects' to be interrogated and their nature has to be forced from them as a kind of confession.

The body I am

The fact that our bodies are things poses an interesting paradox for an existential analyst. My body is a natural thing, but it is also the site of my existence. As a natural thing, my body encounters other things; for example, other human bodies. In turn, my body is encountered by other persons' bodies in its thingly incarnation. As the site of my existence, however, my body is, like my present, not at all a thing. This existential body, which embodies my existence, is not something I have, but something I am. I refer to it as the body I *am*. It often happens that the body I am is precisely not where my natural body is. For example, as I sit waiting for the late arrival of a friend by train, my existence (and, so, the body I am) is there in the coach, which is carrying him toward me but is still many miles away. The body I am is also the embodiment of my possibilities. It 'bodies forth' my existential present. Its most dramatic appearance is in dreams and reverie. By contrast, my natural body (what I refer to as the body I *have*) is a record of my past. It is the body encountered by things.

In the wake of these realizations, I began to experience my own body differently. I became more aware of its dislocations and strivings to be elsewhere or, better, 'elsewhen'. I began to interpret my own and my clients' neuropraxes and paraesthesias differently. I saw peculiar pains and odd sensations as indications, indeed announcements, of the displacement of our embodied existence, rather than as aberrations of the nervous system.

A person's existence is concentrated in the body he is. Much of the time, his existence is evenly dispersed throughout his body, yet it is always localized to some extent. As I type or play the piano, my existence weighs heavily in my arms, and above all at the ends of my fingers. Yet since my body always acts as a whole, when I touch the keyboard, my existence is as much in my mouth and lips, which purse as though I want to say what I merely tap to make appear on the screen or cause the strings to sound on the piano's harp. It is as much in my neck and shoulders, which support the disciplined movements of my fingers. To some extent it is everywhere in my body. At times, the focus is intense, as when I injure a finger or bite my tongue, or in the intensity of orgasm. In general, my existence is mobile in the body I am. There are times, of course, when my existence has vacated my body, and a feeling of numbness or emptiness supervenes; for example, when the beauty of someone I see absorbs my existence and I am entirely there in that person's eyes or on the back of the hand resting next to me. In psychosis, a person's existence may abandon the body he is.

My appreciation for the place of a client's lived body has increased immensely. At times, I even try to feel in my own body where and what he feels. It is one method of working my way into his world. Here I do more than empathize with him. Existential therapy is much more than mental exercise. The notion of the lived body (the body I am) has prominence in my way of thinking about a person's world. Rather than seeing the body as a thing we occupy that carries us along, I think of the body as what lives our existence.

Dancers, whom Martha Graham so felicitously termed 'acrobats of God', have increasingly come to exemplify the way I understand existence. In fact, I have learned a great deal from watching dancers, who have a special knack for embodying their existence. As a result, I have become quite a fan of modern dance, where the choreographic vocabulary is not as restricted as it is in classical dance. I sometimes think of existence as a dance, executed by the body I am, which performs and embodies my possibilities. Like a dancer, my existence may be out of step. Other times, I liken existence to a musician, whose instrument is the body he is. The music he plays is his composition, and he is the composer. Often enough, his performance may be out of tune.

'...poetically man dwells...'

Some years ago, just before I gained an existential perspective on psychotherapy, I had read one of Martin Heidegger's short essays, '. . . poetically man dwells . . .' (Heidegger, 1971). The title is a phrase from a late fragment by Friedrich Hölderlin (1967) that begins 'In lovely blueness blooms the steeple with metal roof . . .'. The complete line from which the title of Heidegger's essay is taken runs 'Full of accomplishment, yet poetically man dwells on this earth.' The fragment is said to reflect Hölderlin's impending madness (schizophrenia), but the profundity of his observation and Heidegger's elucidation of elements of the fragment bring into focus what is for me perhaps the underlying ground of existence that supports our realization of the present and the moments of existential changeover I described earlier. I will conclude with a few thoughts on Hölderlin's observation.

We live through our present, the temporal dimension that always anxiously edges ahead into the future. We are always slightly *en avant* ourselves; and without that edge, we are not fully alive. Existential anxiety describes this disposition. I see existential edginess as an essential part of the poetic nature of life. In excess, of course, anxiety indicates the tendency to want to outwit the future, just as depression indicates an unwillingness (sometimes an inability) to abandon one's past.

What does it mean to live poetically? It means, as Nietzsche says, to create one's life the way an artist creates a work of art. To live poetically is to make a succession of actualities out of a finite set of possibilities. It means carving out one's life with the present edge of existence. To dwell poetically is to constitute a world. Meanings are not handed over to us: we institute them. Piaget understood this quite well in his description of the earliest workings of the intellect, which invents the world in understanding it (Piaget, 1974).

The poetic nature of existence precludes my having a fixed identity, an achievement much touted by psychosocial theory. As someone who will never finally be himself until he dies, I cannot be identified. I am what I am doing at the moment. For example, if I happen to have been trained to play the piano, I am a pianist only when I am at the keyboard, playing. Similarly, I am a writer, but only as long as I continue working at a text. Although I have taught quite regularly for more than 25 years, I am a teacher only when I am in conversation with students. Finally, I have practised as an existential analyst for many years, but I am a psychotherapist only when I am attempting to help someone find his existence.

This is not to say that my identity is dissociated or fragmented, but rather that who I am is what I do, and I am a pianist or a therapist only when I play the piano or talk with someone with therapeutic intention. The contemporary quest is for a single, homogeneous identity in which what I do shifts from moment to moment. I cannot locate the inner sense of sameness that Erik Erikson and others claim is the supreme goal of development (Erikson, 1980). Since the consolidation of identity is supposed to be accomplished by the end of adolescence, perhaps I should admit that I remain in an interminable adolescence or perhaps even in a childhood that rejects the summons to settle on one identity, one fixed persona. I do not find this troubling. I am not insecure about being one thing, then another. Nor do I feel that I am one person playing different roles: that would unnerve me. Instead, I should say that I am potentially many but always only one centre of tailored action and disciplined competence, at times doing this and at other times doing that.

Hölderlin's emphasis on the earth makes his fragment an appropriate epigraph for this essay and for my theoretical perspective. The existential approach has brought my world down to earth. It resonates with the current ecological emphasis and with the critique of technology that moils beneath the surface everywhere. As noted earlier, it is also a value-laden approach. As such, it flies in the face of the prized ideal of the sciences, that theories must remain value-free. We all know that there are no value-free theories (and that natural science is just another religion), but all the same, most clinical psychologists are sceptical about an admittedly value-serious theoretical perspective in their field. Perhaps with good reason, since as psychotherapists we are capable of influencing extremely tender parts of our clients' existence.

Finally, as much as my approach leads away from the naturalistic, it leads me more and more toward nature. I think this is so because, after looking a long time for my existence inside, where the self was said to reside, I have found it out there, among things, between us.

References

Buber, M. (1974) *I and Thou*. New York: Macmillan.

Erikson, E. (1980) *Identity and the Life Cycle*. New York: Norton.

Groth, M. (1982) 'Interpretation for Freud and Heidegger: parataxis and disclosure', *International Review of Psycho-Analysis* **9**, 67–74.

Heidegger, M. (1962) *Being and Time*. San Francisco: Harper San Francisco.

Heidegger, M. (1969) *Discourse on Thinking*. New York: Harper.

Heidegger, M. (1971) *Poetry, Language, Thought*. New York: Harper.

Heron, J. (1970) 'The phenomenology of social encounter: the gaze', *Philosophy and Phenomenological Research* **31**, 243–64.

Hölderlin, F. (1967) *Poems and Fragments*. Ann Arbor: University of Michigan Press.

Lane, H. (1979) *The Wild Boy of Aveyron*. Cambridge: Harvard University Press.

Piaget, J. (1974) *To Understand Is to Invent*. New York: Viking Press.

Plato (1961) 'Meno', *The Collected Dialogues of Plato*. Princeton: Princeton University Press.

Swift, J. (1726) *Gulliver's Travels*. New York: Houghton Mifflin, 1960.
van den Berg, J. (1971) 'Phenomenology and metabletics', *Humanitas*
   VII (3).
Wolfe, T. (1989) *You Can't Go Home Again*. New York: Harper.

7 | The Desire and Pursuit of the Whole (Analytical Psychology)

Anthony Stevens

> To live is to battle with trolls in the vaults of heart and brain.
> To write: that is to sit in judgement over one's self.
>
> (Henrik Ibsen)

To ask an analyst to say how he embodies his theories in his life is to dangle before him the temptation to present himself as a paragon of what his own school of analysis can achieve. Not to be seduced by this demands the self-discipline of a night security guard at Harrods: he must not expropriate goods that do not belong to him.

As an introvert who grew up as an only child, my most important experiences have been inner ones, and I have always tended to keep them to myself. The task of self-revelation imposed by this chapter is not, therefore, easily met. At first I was reluctant even to attempt it, but as I lived with the idea I became intrigued by its challenge. The extent to which one embodies one's theories in one's own life is, I suppose, a measure of one's integrity. The analyst who applies one set of assumptions to his patients and another to himself is at best a hypocrite and at worst a charlatan. To do genuine work you have to ensure that knowledge connects with life.

At the same time, there is a place for scepticism. Is it really healthy to *embody* one's theory? Certainly, one should live it sufficiently to explore its full implications, but one should also be able to stand back from it, test it, and see where it doesn't work.

What is more, my training as a doctor, psychiatrist and experimental psychologist has made me critically aware that all schools of analysis actually *disembody* the psyche. They still talk as if 'the ghost' were independent of 'the machine'. For me, body and psyche are inseparable. They are two aspects of the same process. You cannot have one without the other, and both are equally the result of evolution. Jung's theory of archetypes attempts to embrace this fact, and the books I have written over the last twenty years have all examined the significance of archetypes for analytic practice and for life. While my academic training has given me the highest respect for the empirical method of scientific enquiry, I regard personal embodiment in life as the greatest experiment of all. Ultimately, life is not a mechanism to be analysed and explained, but a miracle to be lived.

Temperamentally, I think, I must be a congenital Jungian, for I seem to have been born with a mind that delights in observing itself, and I share Jung's 'passionate urge to understanding' which he described as the strongest element in his nature. Quite early in life I formed the opinion that the most fascinating pursuit possible was the psychological investigation of oneself, and when I read Jung's memoir, *Memories, Dreams, Reflections* (1963), I felt a sense of homecoming and of close kinship with Jung. This feeling has not left me: it has cast its glow on every aspect of my life. I was particularly reassured by Jung's revelation that he experienced himself as having two personalities, which he called 'No. 1' and 'No. 2' respectively. I had experienced inner dialogues between aspects of myself since early childhood, and had come to fear this was abnormal. Jung (and my analysis) helped me to realize how highly creative such self-communion could be.

The single most important fact about Jung was his introspective genius. Through rigorous self-examination, and what can only be described as a religious commitment to his inner life, he was able to enter that largely inaccessible hinterland of the human spirit where all meanings and all feelings originate.

By turning inwards, he, the individual man, was able to reveal the universal man lurking in his own nature. He wrote down and painted what he experienced and related it to what others had discovered before him – Plato, Aristotle, Spinoza, Locke, and Schopenhauer, as well as the *Naturphilosophen*, the Taoists and the alchemists – and, as he did so, found that his personality underwent a series of transformations which he felt promoted his own development as a human being. This became for me a model to which I readily and quite naturally adapted. And that, I believe, is what it means to call oneself a Jungian. Jung is as much a figure of inspiration, a model of how to proceed, as he is a source of knowledge and of insight.

A major attraction of Jung's legacy is a lack of dogma. It does not require one to squint at the phenomena of human existence through some narrow theoretical keyhole. His formulations were never definitive or final. The golden rule of Jungian psychology is that there are no golden rules. The only man who really embodied Jungian theory was Jung himself. Analytical psychology is truly *his* psychology: it is an extension of his own personality. When Jung's followers discuss what it means to be a Jungian, they invariably mention one of his most quoted quips: 'Thank God I'm Jung,' he said, 'and not a Jungian!' He was clearly ambivalent about the teacher–disciple relationship. He liked having disciples but he also found them a bit of a nuisance. He was hostile to the idea of establishing a training institute and only got round to allowing it in old age because, he said, his followers would seize the opportunity to set one up between his death and his funeral, and, on the whole, he felt the result might be less disastrous if he had a hand in it. The last thing he wanted was for his students to become replicas of himself or to turn his ideas into a creed to be learnt by heart. Rather, he advised them to make use of the techniques he had devised to pursue their own 'individuation' – that is, to discover their own truth, to become *themselves*, to become as whole and complete a human being as their circumstances would allow. In this, too, he was perpetuating an ancient tradition. When, for example, the classical Greek poet, Pindar, advised: 'Become what thou art', he meant: 'Abandon your superficial persona, your social clichés, and follow the Delphic injunction to "know thyself" – to discover the full humanity latent in your soul and to befriend the personal daimon residing there.' Both Plato and Aristotle taught that to become your true self is to make explicit what implicitly you already are. This was essentially Jung's position.

In any Jungian training the crucial didactic experience is the personal analysis, not so that the candidate will become brainwashed with a set of dogmas and practices, but so as to learn how to work creatively with the unconscious psyche. Only when embarked on the process oneself is it possible to help others along the same path of discovery. This is one of the few things about which Jung was adamant:

> The analyst must go on learning endlessly, and never forget that each new case brings problems to light and thus gives rise to unconscious assumptions that have never before been constellated. We could say, without too much exaggeration, that a good half of every treatment that probes at all deeply consists in the doctor's examining himself, for only what he can put right in himself can he hope to put right in the patient. It is no loss, either, if he feels that the patient is hitting him, or even scoring off him: it is his own hurt that gives the measure of his power to heal. This, and nothing else, is the meaning of the Greek myth of the wounded physician. (CW16, para. 239)

To take this to heart means shouldering a heavy responsibility, but it also makes the work of a committed therapist one of the most challenging and rewarding professions it is possible to embrace.

Inevitably, in the course of training one becomes familiar with classical Jungian concepts – the archetypes of the collective unconscious, the anima and animus, the persona, shadow, and the Self, as well as the theory of psychological types and the principle of individuation – and these become part of one's intellectual equipment. They are meaningful only when intimately related to one's own experience and worked into one's own scheme of things. To a certain extent, as Chekov said, 'man is what he believes'. But, ultimately, there is no such creature as a Jungian. There is only the Self and what one makes of it.

Although my personal analysis ended over 35 years ago, I still work with my own material in the way I learnt then. I keep a journal to commemorate each day as it passes so that events are not lost, and transitory ideas and experiences do not sink uncherished into the maw of the unconscious. To enjoy each day is a prime duty. For too many of us life is what passes while we work for a future that never arrives. Keeping a journal is a ritual celebration of life. My dreams are still indispensable to me because every night they put me in touch with the emotionally charged memories of which my complexes are made, and, when I work at them, help to liberate the archetypal potential trapped in them. This is sometimes frightening work, for complexes can be disruptive of one's peace of mind. Jung compared them to 'the hobgoblins of folklore who go crashing about the house at night'. However much we may wish to get free of them, our complexes are us: they are the bones and sinews of the personal psyche; they provide the armature round which our personal identity is built. To tamper with these vital structures can threaten the security of one's very existence. They have to be handled with care. A lifetime engaged in this activity – not only in myself but in working with my patients – has brought home to me that, in order to pass as sane, we all censure our own madness, confining our psychotic life to the asylum of our dreams. But, properly managed, it is a safe asylum, a temenos of healing and creativeness, in which all the crucial transformations of life proceed. Dreams are essential ingredients of our psychobiological reality. They owe their origins and contents as much to our evolutionary history as a species as to our personal history as individuals. This gives them their endlessly fascinating quality.

Vital processes going on at the unconscious level constantly work towards the integration and nourishment of the total personality, and I frequently catch glimpses of this in hypnagogic images as well as dreams. Even during wakefulness seminal thoughts and images slip in and out of consciousness like the sun in a cloudy sky. This daily and nightly communion with the Self is the primary datum of my life. Though I love good company, I love solitude no less, for one is never alone with the Self. On solitary walks on the moors, along the seashore, through meadows and beside woodland streams, this inner personality is one's loyalest companion, best friend, and most trusted confidant. As Anthony Storr pointed out in his book on solitude (Storr, 1989), modern psychotherapy has placed an almost compulsive emphasis on the capacity of individuals to make mature relationships on equal terms. Achievement of this capacity is adopted uncritically as *the* criterion of emotional maturity. But, says Storr, psychotherapy has failed to recognize that emotional maturity is no less reflected in the capacity to be creatively alone. 'The happiest lives', he wrote, 'are probably those in which neither interpersonal relationships nor impersonal interests are idealised as the only way to salvation. The desire and pursuit of the whole must comprehend both aspects of human nature.'

It is out of the inner relationship to the Self that I have written books such as *Archetype, The Two Million-Year-Old Self*, and *Private Myths*. In some ways my relation to the Self resembles W. H. Auden's description of a poet's marriage to his muse: sometimes it is happy and sometimes life with her is difficult. In my marriage to the Self we have our ups and downs but on the whole it is rich and we share vivid moments of poetry. To be elated by the sudden intrusion of an inspired idea has on me something of the same effect as Westminster Bridge or daffodils on Wordsworth. Like poetry, books on psychology cannot be written to order. One waits, in John Betjeman's phrase, for something to come through from 'the Management upstairs', and the Management can be very capricious. But one can't write much of value without it. Since my life is now mainly devoted to writing, I find the relationship with my unconscious irreplaceable.

On one occasion, for example, the whole structure of a book was given to me in a dream. It occurred while I was writing *On Jung* (1990). For some weeks I had been struggling with the problem of how best to present the relationship between Jung's life and the development of his ideas. Then one morning I awoke from a dream in which I had seen a rainbow ascending out of mist in a great parabola. Towards its summit it became brilliantly coloured, but as it fell back to earth the colours gradually began to fade. As I gazed at it, the rainbow divided longitudinally into three separate rainbows, describing closely related arcs across the sky, one above the other. Even in my dream I knew this was about my book. Fully awake, I pondered the significance of the dream, and its meaning came to me in a flash. The rainbow represented the human life cycle, ascending out of the unconscious mists of infancy to the richly coloured prime of life and then descending into the more pastel shaded years of late maturity. But why were there three of them? Here again the meaning struck me with great clarity. The lowest rainbow represented the archetypal stages of the life cycle through which all human individuals pass; the middle rainbow represented Jung's personal experience of the life cycle (his biography); while the uppermost rainbow represented the psychological insights that emerged as he lived through each stage. I at once set to work organizing my material in accordance with this plan, each chapter reflecting the tripartite division suggested by my rainbow dream. *On Jung* remains, I think, the best structured of my books.

Enjoyment of solitude does not preclude the joys and pains of relationship. I have lived with the same companion for over 30 years, which isn't bad going nowadays. We have restored an ancient house in Devon in a region of great natural beauty and, with much expert help, created a garden which brings peace and happiness to ourselves, our families and friends. The success of our relationship owes little to the theories of analysis and much to the power of tolerance. As Fielding put it, there is no greater folly than to seek to correct the natural infirmities of those we love. Tolerance and love combined with respect for each other's privacy is the key. A good marriage, wrote Rainer Maria Rilke, is that in which each appoints the other guardian of his solitude!

I am not sure how far being an analyst affects how I relate to people. Certainly I don't set out to analyse friends and acquaintances, but I am often aware of subplots playing in the background of their lives. I find myself listening to what they say with a third ear, so to speak, that often picks up the things they don't say more acutely than the things they do. I tend to be an attentive listener, my imagination continues to play as they talk to intuit where their thoughts could be leading. But I am not convinced that you have to be an analyst to do that. After all, novelists must do it all the time.

As an introvert I am less interested in the actual world than in how I feel and respond to it. In itself, reality is meaningless: it's what one makes of it in the psyche that matters. Similarly, my link to other people is through their feelings and thoughts rather than how they behave. As a result, I have little interest in politics and find the clamorous squabbling between left and right a bore. I have loved the analytic relationship because it is a richly creative process of discovery – halfway between what goes on in the mind when one is alone (focused on inner thoughts and feelings) and what goes on in the company of others (focused on what I think they are thinking and feeling). Underlying this communion is our shared humanity, enshrined in the symbolic images and archetypal experiences of the collective unconscious – which, for me, is no mere hypothesis but an empirical reality implicit in every moment of human existence.

That Jung appealed to me so deeply is because, unlike the Freudian, Kleinian and objective relations analysts, he stressed the central importance of the introverted condition and had an infinitely more profound conception of the Self. To practitioners of other schools, the self is a personal, autobiographical construct, whereas to Jung, the Self is endowed with all the evolved psychological potential of our species. One is not the creator but the custodian of the Self. As a consequence, Jung's perception is Janus-headed: it sees both the personal and the transpersonal at the same time. While we are all different we are also all the same. I share this double vision. By birth and upbringing I am an Englishman, but I experience myself as a citizen of the world. I am both a man of the present and a man of all time. At the core of my being there is little to distinguish me from stone-age man. That could be why I feel most at home in the heart of Dartmoor, or in a sailing boat at sea, where there is nothing to remind me of the century I happen to be living in.

As I look back on my professional life, I realize how richly sustained it has been by the evolutionary-archetypal perspective on human nature, for it has provided me with that precious commodity – indispensable to the well-being of mental health practitioners and their patients – *therapeutic optimism*. Instead of viewing a patient's situation as the result of 'illness', one sees it as the result of a potentially healthy personality struggling to meet the demands of life. Knowing that each human being is endowed with the archetypal potential of the species gives one confidence that, however disordered an individual's psychological development may be, the *potential* for further growth and better adaptation is still there, implicit in the psychophysical structure of the organism. Successful therapeutic outcome, as I conceive it, depends on mobilizing archetypal components of the phylogenetic psyche by encouraging patients to dream, to fantasize, to paint, to open themselves to relationships with new friends and acquaintances and to find new ways of relating to old ones, as well as becoming conscious of the strategies and conflicts that have been controlling their lives in the past. To make headway in such demanding work, one has to develop one's own creative abilities if one hopes to do much more than patch up one's patients and enable them to go on existing. This is a major reason why I have loved the work. It is a two-way process through which both participants help each other to grow.

But on withdrawing from work with patients one has to beware of the seductive power of solitude. As Jung said, 'you cannot individuate on Everest'. Individuation is not about being self-centred (i.e. wallowing in the ego), but about bringing the Self to consciousness, and the Self requires a social matrix in which to be actualized. In Jung's view, good relations with other people grow out of good relations with the Self: 'individuation does not shut one out from the world, but gathers the world to oneself' (CW8, para. 432). In our extraverted, materialistic culture this may require you to risk appearing eccentric, for in Western society it is often hard to be both conventional and alive. To be strictly 'normal' is to be 'cabin'd, cribb'd, confin'd' – the aspiration of those who have lost their way. 'Bring me a normal man,' said Jung, 'and I will cure him.' To succeed as a writer, for example, it is essential to observe one's natural rhythms and flow with them. I get sleepy by 9.30 in the evening and so I go to bed. I wake up alert and full of ideas at about 3.30 a.m., so I put on a dressing gown, make some coffee, and return to bed. There I begin writing, and if all goes well, continue writing till 7 or 8. Then I break for some exercise and, twice a week, weather permitting, I run four miles round a beautiful lake not far from where I live. After a shower, more coffee and some fruit, I resume work until 11 or 12.

I particularly love the early hours because they guarantee total seclusion. No telephones, no knocks on the door, no distractions. Just peace and freedom to concentrate. Nearly everything I have written I have done in bed. It is a womb in which I nurture embryonic ideas and bring them tentatively to birth. I don't type. I need a pen in my hand to shape and focus my thoughts as they rise into consciousness. When I have completed the morning's stint, I record it on tape, and send it to my secretary, who is a wizard with a word processor. She sends it back and the next day I edit what she has done, add to it, play with it, and alter it, sometimes out of all recognition. It is a process I greatly enjoy and, fortunately, my secretary is a kind and patient woman. After an early lunch I sleep for an hour or so and then either go to the gym with a colleague or for a long walk with my dog. If I have any supervising or teaching to do I prefer to arrange it for the late afternoon.

Though I find deep contentment in my own company, I also love the society of friends and colleagues, especially in the evening and preferably at home, when my extraverted side blossoms in the context of wine and food. Since we live in a corner of the country remote from London, we like to have people to stay. For most of the day we all do our own thing, then we meet up at meal times and for walks. Thanks to their unfailing good nature, friends seem ready enough to indulge my need to retire early and to pass the morning in the seclusion of my bedroom, and no one rings me up after 9.30 p.m. or between 1.30 and 3 in the afternoon, my somewhat unusual hours of sleep.

Since I hit 60 I have steadily reduced the hours I devote to analysis. I have not taken on any new patients in the last five years and now only occasionally see old ones who need a top-up session to do some work on an important dream or to discuss some issue that has cropped up in their lives. Though I miss the work, I enjoy the freedom from responsibility that retirement brings. Most of all I relish that most blissful of states – an empty diary. Diary-observance is the self-imposed tyranny of the professional classes. Freedom from it makes it possible to adjust my life to the weather, which is a great contribution to happiness if one lives in the south-west of England. If it rains I work; when the sun shines I drop everything and head off for the moors or the sea. The loss of commitment to patients also makes it easier to spend more time abroad, especially in France, Italy and Greece, which of all the countries of the world I love the most, partly for their physical beauty, their climate and their people, but mostly for their architecture, their history and their art. Exploring the roots of our culture feeds the individuation process, for it heightens one's awareness of the immense privilege of being human and of how enormous is the creative vitality of our kind.

As I get older, I become less preoccupied with events in the contemporary world and more interested in what has always been true of human existence. Consequently, I spend little time reading newspapers, and even less watching television, preferring to immerse myself in literature, art and music which speak to the 'eternal' human condition. It is curious that when we have passed our years of reproductive usefulness, nature allows us to stay around for a further 30 or 40 years before finally gathering us to her bosom. I wonder, is it because she is lazy, or is there method in her mildness? Jung was sure there was a purpose: 'a human being would certainly not grow to be seventy or eighty years old if this longevity had no meaning for the species. The afternoon of life must have a significance of its own and cannot be merely a pitiful appendage to life's morning' (CW8, para. 787). The function of people in the second half of life, he argued, is to sustain the culture that supported their youth. He saw the goal of old age as not senility but wisdom. Unfortunately, our youth-obsessed culture no longer sees it like that. The wisdom of age is not valued because knowledge is now assumed to reside in technology. This is a disastrous conceptual error. However well educated the young may be, hours spent on the Internet can never provide the inspiration to be gained from personal contact with someone who *knows* and has *lived*. To individuate is to realize one's existence as a unique expression of humanity and, within the frail vessel of one's little psychic world, to distil the essence of creation.

As a Jungian, I see old age as a time for reflection, for assimilation of the past, a time to search for meaning and to move towards wholeness. If we are to make a success of our later years, we have to learn to bear the process of ageing with equanimity, to come to terms with death and to experience our co-existence with all creation. To 'become what thou art' is to make explicit what implicitly one already is. This means overcoming the divisions imposed by the parental and cultural milieu, to divest oneself of the false wrappings of the persona, abandon one's ego-defences and, rather than projecting one's shadow onto others, strive to know it and acknowledge it as part of one's inner life, and attempt to bring to conscious fulfilment the intentions of the Self. Complete achievement of these objectives within the compass of one individual lifetime is never possible, of course, but that is not the point. 'The goal is important only as an idea,' wrote Jung, 'the essential thing is the opus which leads to the goal: *that* is the goal of a lifetime' (CW16, para. 400).

Quite possibly it is in the practice of analysis that the wisdom of age finds its most valuable expression in the contemporary world. Analysts get better as they grow older, both as practitioners and as teachers, and there are many examples of people doing excellent work well into their seventies and eighties. Our culture has been compulsively adolescent for so long that it must be due for an *enantiodromia*, a swing over to its opposite. The survival of more and more people into healthy old age means they can make a cultural contribution of enormous significance. Unfortunately, many find the collective emphasis on youth intimidating. Rather than voicing a critical assessment of what is happening to our cultural values, they keep silent for fear of being ridiculed as reactionary or of becoming 'Disgusted of Tunbridge Wells'. This will change as older people begin to discover their increasing political and economic power, and, eventually, the cultural pendulum will swing in their direction. This is all to the good, for it is important in the war of the generations that neither side should win. The accumulated treasury of tested experience which constitutes the very fabric of human culture can never become obsolete between one generation and the next. In all human communities a balance has to be achieved between the traditional forces of conservation and the progressive forces of change. This knowledge gives me the courage to go on writing and teaching out of my experience and standing up for what I believe to be true. Experience is precious, after all, because it is something we have truly earned. We have paid for it with the coin of life and have emptied a purse that cannot be refilled. But it is important not to become pompous or self-righteous about it, especially when lecturing or conducting seminars. One must avoid what Lord Halifax called 'the vanity of teaching', which, he said, 'tempteth a man to forget he is a blockhead!'

The quest for meaning and the play of ideas continue to hold me in thrall, but as I grow older I become more preoccupied with the *aesthetics* of living – not just the appreciation of music, architecture and art, but the intense feeling response engendered by the way things are, the sheer miracle of existence. This is the point at which aesthetic, scientific and religious modes of responding overlap. Albert Einstein called it 'the most beautiful emotion'. It arises when one responds to the world, contemplates what lies beyond our immediate sensory perceptions, and experiences the thrill of meaningful discovery. Such a moment occurred one summer evening when I stood on the cliffs of North Cornwall near Bedruthan Steps, watching the sun set over a vast expanse of sea. The scene induced in me the same involuntary sense of awe in the presence of infinity which millions of human beings must have felt since our species came into existence. I was having what Rudolf Otto called a 'numinous' experience and, at that precise moment, *I* was having it *for humanity*. The primordial human being – the 'two-million-year-old Self' – was seeing the Atlantic through my eyes. This was the *phrike* which the Greeks recognized as the hair-raising shudder, the sacred spine-tingling shiver of awe and dread, which is the quintessence of numinous excitement. It arises from unconscious dynamics in the Self; it is not something that can be induced through conscious exercise of the will.

Another such moment occurred with my first real understanding of the grandeur of Jung's concept of the archetype and the immensity of its implications. I felt like Archimedes as he jumped out of his bath. I had discovered an ultimate truth, and it was to provide me with the source of my life's work. By excavating and 'amplifying' the archetype, I was committing myself to what really mattered: I was studying the psychic aspect of the human genome. Everything I have written has been driven by that knowledge.

Though he died 40 years ago, Jung still has a great appeal to people whose spiritual needs are no longer satisfied by established religion. Jung's whole life was an expression of a truly protestant quest – a spiritual journey away from the moribund church of his clergyman father to encounter the living God as a personal revelation in the Self. He believed that by committing himself to his individuation through engaging the symbols emerging from dreams and 'active imagination' he was not merely extending his own consciousness but enabling God to become more conscious of what he created! 'That is the meaning of divine service, of the service which man can render to God, that the Creator may become conscious of his creation, and man conscious of himself' (Jung, 1963).

Though I do not share Jung's belief in a personal God who needs me to make Him conscious of His own Creation, I readily embrace Jung's insight that behind our purely personal intelligence a deeper, transpersonal intelligence is at work. I do not see this as 'God' but as the evolved potential of human nature implicit in the Self. The realization of this potential in consciousness represents both a personal and a biological achievement. For, as Huxley observed, with the evolution of consciousness the cosmos has become conscious of itself.

Darwin was an earlier source of inspiration to me than Jung. When I was 10 or 11, our scripture master was expounding Genesis as *the* correct explanation of our origins. At the same time, the BBC was broadcasting a series of radio programmes on evolutionary biology for schools called *How Things Began*. As we were never exposed to these programmes at school, I played truant – with my mother's collusion – so that I could listen to them. Since then I have come to see evolution by natural selection as the 'creation myth' of our time. The main difference between Darwin's 'myth' and all the other creation myths human populations have produced is that Darwin's is demonstrably true. What is more, no other creation myth is as stupendous, for it has taken three billion years to unfold. It surpasses the Genesis story in grandeur and just as surely opens up a way into the sacred. Appreciation of the miraculous immensity of Darwin's account makes one realize how precious and extraordinary is every living thing. The wonder of the whole Darwinian epic is that what originally consisted of a clump of replicating molecules in the 'primordial soup' became capable of writing Shakespearean sonnets, building Chartres Cathedral, composing Don Giovanni, painting the Sistine Chapel, putting a man on the moon, and devising analytical psychology. It is creative use of our evolved capacities that makes these achievements possible.

The union of Darwinian and Jungian insights has provided me with the greatest source of inspiration both as a clinician and a writer. It has rendered the archetype numinous for me. And I now consider myself to be as much an evolutionary psychiatrist as a Jungian analyst. Not only does evolutionary psychology provide a sound empirical basis for Jung's view of the unconscious as made up of archetypal propensities (evolutionary psychologists call them 'evolved psychological mechanisms'), but it invites analytical psychology to participate in the major paradigm shift that is occurring in the behavioural sciences (Stevens, 1998, 2000, 2001; Stevens and Price, 2000). That the different schools of therapy, founded on the assumptions of their charismatic leaders, have degenerated into exclusive and mutually hostile 'sects' is because these assumptions have largely escaped objective verification. But this state of affairs cannot last. As research into psychotherapeutic practice proceeds and we learn more about 'what works for whom' (Roth and Fonagy, 1996), differences between the various schools will be eroded and a new theoretical synthesis will emerge. My own belief is that the evolutionary-archetypal perspective can provide a rich nucleus round which all theoretical approaches can muster, and I hope that in the sunshine that is left to me, I shall be able to make some small contribution to this achievement.

References

Jung, C. G. (1953–78) Sources of quotations from *The Collected Works of C. G. Jung*, edited by H. Read, M. Fordham and G. Adler and published in London by Routledge, are indicated by the volume number followed by the number of the paragraph from which the quotation is taken, e.g. CW16, para. 239.

Jung, C. G. (1963) *Memories, Dreams, Reflections*. London: Routledge & Kegan Paul; New York: Random House.

Roth, A. and Fonagy, P. (1996) *What Works for Whom? A Critical Review of Psychotherapy Research*. New York: The Guildford Press.

Stevens, A. (1990) *On Jung*. London: Routledge. Revised edition published by Penguin in paperback and by the Princeton University Press in 1999.

Stevens, A. (1998) *An Intelligent Person's Guide to Psychotherapy*. London: Duckworth.

Stevens, A. (2000) 'Jungian analysis and evolutionary psychotherapy: an integrative approach', in P. Gilbert and K. C. Bailey (eds) *Genes on the Couch: Explorations in Evolutionary Psychotherapy*. London: Brunner-Routledge.

Stevens, A. (2001) 'The status of archetypal theory', in R. Withers (ed.) *Controversies in Analytical Psychology*. Hove: The Psychology Press.

Stevens, A. and Price, J. (2000) *Evolutionary Psychiatry: A New Beginning* (second edition). London: Routledge.

Storr, A. (1989) *Solitude*. London: HarperCollins.

8 | Authenticity in Action (Humanistic–Integrative Psychotherapy)

John Rowan

THE CRISIS that started me off in 1970 was the failure (as I saw it) of a group I was running. It was an experiential group of an experimental nature, which had started off with about fifteen people coming every week, and had tailed off to three people after six months (Rowan, 1989). So I started off with the programme of finding out why groups live and die. My crisis was not very emotional, because at that stage I was not an emotional person, but was rather of the nature of curiosity. I was a social psychologist, and supposed to know about groups, but felt I knew very little. I was involved mainly in consumer research; I ran large surveys and small psychological investigations, and went to conferences and gave papers. I was also active in the Social Psychology Section of the BPS, and even organized a conference for them. In the evenings I was involved in the arts – poetry in particular – often in collaboration with a marvellous poet and artist named Bob Cobbing.

There had been all kinds of precursors and preparations for the journey I was about to take. I had read philosophy, such as Spinoza and Hegel; I had read Zen Buddhism, such as Christmas Humphreys, Alan Watts, Paul Reps, Lawrence Ferlinghetti and Philip Kapleau; I had read theology in Anders Nygren and mysticism in Evelyn Underhill; I had read the poems and stories of Jack Kerouac, William Burroughs and Allen Ginsberg, and written original poetry of my own; I had learned from

Harold Walsby and George Walford how to think dialectically. I had been through the 1960s. I had tried LSD, and had had what I would describe as a mystical experience. I was 45 years old.

The first workshop I ever went to in my investigation of the world of groups was quite a large one, held in the Forester's Hall in Kentish Town. It was led by a man and a woman, and consisted of a number of experiential exercises, some in the large group, some in small groups and some in pairs. I found it exciting and absorbing. For the first time I started to make connections between action and emotion. It was as if my feelings became real things worth paying attention to. At first it was all quite confusing. It was a jumble of things rather than a consistent or coherent story. But soon there was a conference of the recently formed Association for Humanistic Psychology in Britain, and I made a lot of personal contacts which convinced me that humanistic psychology was just what I was looking for. I invited myself to a committee meeting and within two years was in the Chair of the organization.

One of my most interesting discoveries was about the pathology of autonomy. At first, one of the attractions of the humanistic approach for me was its emphasis on autonomy. I was already very good, I thought, on autonomy; I felt quite superior on that score. But the truth of the matter was that I did not have autonomy at all. What I had was what Reich, Lowen, Fairbairn, Johnson and Lake call a schizoid defence system. In other words, I was rather distant and private and emotionally shut down. This was partly, and perhaps mainly, because in my first 30 years I had lived in 30 different places, and to avoid feeling upset at leaving people, places, pets and toys I had developed a protective defence of not getting attached to them. It was this enforced and pathological independence that I had mistaken for autonomy. Faced with a problem, my tendency was to withdraw. And it was only by being challenged about this, sometimes painfully, in group after group that I began to see through it. And this confirmed for me that I was in the right place, that the humanistic approach offered the best way for me to develop as a human being. This was a slow process – it did not happen at once. It was painful for me to realize that I had been kidding myself all these years, and I resisted this knowledge for as long as I could.

I read a lot, and talked to people, and went to workshops, and the story that emerged was that I was supposed to find my centre. I was supposed to move from peripheral and largely phony things like the self-image, the false self, the unreal self, the adapted child, the persona, the mind split from body and so forth, to the self, the true self, the real self, the free child, the Self, the bodymind unity, and so on (see Figure 8.1). I had to give up my illusions, my compulsions and my social conditioning, and move on up the Maslovian ladder.

But this was a frightening task. It was frightening because it appeared to me as if I had to abandon and leave behind

	Central	Peripheral
C. G. Jung	Self	Persona
A. Adler	Creative self	Guiding fiction
P. Federn	Id	Ego-states
F. S. Perls	Self	Self-image
R. Assagioli	I	Subpersonalities
D. W. Winnicott	True self	False self
H. Guntrip	Primary libidinal ego	Internal objects
R. D. Laing	Real self	False self
A. Janov	Real self	Unreal self
J. Love	Primal intent	Conscious will
R. E. Johnson	Real self	Symbolic self
P. Koestenbaum	Transcendental ego	Empirical ego

Figure 8.1 Chart showing many versions of the contrast between what is inner and what is outer.

something that had served me in good stead for 45 years (my ego), in favour of something I was supposed to have but which seemed by comparison to be weak, thin, uncertain, shaky, mysterious, wispy – something of which I had no experience at all (my real self). It was a very uncomfortable place to be. I had dreams of standing on the edge of a precipice, and eventually I jumped, but it took several years.

One encouraging experience which helped me along the path was reading Barry Stevens (1970). In her book *Don't Push the River* she seemed to be actually speaking and acting from the position of being a fully functioning human being. I found I could learn from her something more of what it was like to be a spontaneous and creative human being. She didn't tell me how to be, she just told me how she was herself. She was a powerful role-model, or better still non-role-model, for me.

I started to have glimpses of what it would be like to be real. One important one was at a Carl Rogers workshop in 1971. It was the first such workshop to be held in London, I believe. It was in about November, and I had just broken up with the woman I had been living with for a year. I was feeling completely down and dark and empty – it was one of the worst times in my life.

One of the exercises in this workshop was that four people sat at the corners of a large table. Four other people sat with them. The task was to be real with the other person for ten minutes. Then the outer four moved round to the next corner, to be real for another ten minutes. There were four meetings altogether. When I got to my third meeting, I met a woman who could only talk about her sister. She was very moved, and went very deeply into her feelings. At the end of the ten minutes she said she had got further in that ten minutes than she had in the previous two years of her therapy.

This taught me that you don't have to feel good to be real. Indeed it may be the case that the more vulnerable the therapist is, the more vulnerable that may allow the client to be. Perhaps you can't be real and defensive at the same time. Of course I wasn't as clear about it then as I am now, but it was a striking lesson all the same.

Entering the Centaur stage

One of the first groups I went to in 1970 was a gestalt group at Quaesitor, which at that time was just a basement room in St John's Wood. We sat round on cushions in a circle. At one point the group leader said, 'Now, let's just go round and say how you are feeling right now.' When it came to my turn I could only say I had no idea. I didn't know if I was feeling anything, never mind which particular feeling I might be having. If I had the same experience now, I would simply say 'I feel blocked' – but I didn't even have that language then. So I began to cultivate my feelings and get in touch with them more. The first one to come was anger. Then came grief. Then came love; that was a painful lesson, and I wrote a series of poems about it. Then came pain. Then came fear.

I think someone could have a complete set of feelings and still not be in touch with their real self, but it is a necessary step on the way to being a whole person.

I should say that one of the most important helps to discovering my feelings was co-counselling. I learned co-counselling in 1973 as part of an innovative Diploma in Applied Behavioural Science I was doing at the Polytechnic of North London under John Southgate. I went to a residential week led by Harvey Jackins, and later learned three other forms of co-counselling. It is almost ideal for learning about emotions, and that was what I needed most at that time. I explored the limits of my anger, and found that it was not as huge as I had imagined. I went into my grief and sadness, and cried buckets – in fact I remember crying about the sadness of all my unshed tears! I owned up to my pain, and really allowed myself to experience it to the full. I remember one session where I puzzled and puzzled about love. Was it possible to love everyone, or was love something very special which only meant something if it were reserved for the special person? In the end I decided it was possible to love everyone, and this was a very important insight for me. One of the characteristics of the Centaur stage (Ken Wilber's label for the humanistic and existential level of consciousness), I think, is that there is no withholding there. And that goes with the non-defensive character of the real self. The mental ego constantly needs defending, but the real self doesn't. And it was a real relief to me to discover, little by little, that I could give up defensiveness.

One of the important early experiences was the experiencing of my own death. In 1971, during a group experience, I enacted my own death. I lay on the middle of the floor, was covered up with a sheet, and people started to talk about me as if I were dead. I went through a very powerful experience, cried a great deal, and really had the feeling that I had experienced death. My feeling was of having gone to the end, of having hit the ultimate bottom. After that I felt a sense of liberation, as if I didn't have to worry about death, because I had already been through it. Again I am not saying that this is an essential part of the Centaur stage, but it certainly helped. This theme of death and rebirth was to come back more than once in later times.

All through this period I was losing my self-image; both the positive self-image of a good provider and an interesting person, and my negative image of being a superior and arrogant person, a sexual failure, an emotional incompetent and a male oppressor.

This was helped by my discovery of the idea of subpersonalities, which grew in me all through this period, although I didn't put it into writing very much until ten years later. It was in 1972 that I went to a group led by Jay Stattman, which he called a Symboldrama group, and got in touch with some of my subpersonalities. It felt like a new world opening up – something I had not thought about before. I felt as if my creativity had been given a new set of tools to work with. It was like an opening of my psyche into a whole room I had not known was there. Later I did some work in psychosynthesis, and came across the idea of subpersonalities all over again. My experience of the gradual movement of my subpersonalities was crucial to the whole process. For example, one of the early discoveries was a little girl, who was the only one of my subpersonalities to be lovable; but when I found that I could be lovable, the little girl dropped out. Similarly, one of the early discoveries was Brown Cow, who used to lead groups; but when I became a more authentic group leader, Brown Cow disappeared.

I think it is important to say that I went through the classical elements in any complete psychotherapy, but not in what might be considered the right order. I did my Kleinian stuff about the bad breast before I did my birth and my mother stuff, and my mother stuff before doing my Oedipal stuff. I did my Oedipal stuff before my father stuff. I did my father stuff before doing my womb stuff. I did my womb stuff before doing my schizoid stuff. I did my schizoid stuff before doing my past-life stuff. I did my past-life stuff before I did my implantation stuff. I think they were all necessary, but they did not come in any logical order, it seems to me. All this work taught me that I was just as neurotic, just as psychotic, as anyone else. I was superior to no one. This was a very important realization for me. Of all the work I did, the most important to me was the course in Primal Integration led by Bill Swartley at the end of the 1970s. This is the very heartland of my theoretical approach. And it has seemed to me since that it is the primal work, and the cathartic work in therapy, which makes the most difference to the way people live their lives.

After being in a number of groups, I had an experience of contacting my real self. This was after a catharsis during which I healed one of the splits in my consciousness. This I consider to be a mystical experience, and although it was only a glimpse, it was for me very important, as the authors of *Spiritual Choices* say it can be (Anthony *et al.*, 1987). The experience did not last, and I could not get it back by an effort of will, but I went to more groups and had the experience again and again. Gradually, over the next few years, I became able to contact my real self at will, and to relate authentically with other people from that position. This contact with the real self, which has been described so well by many people in the humanistic tradition (Bugental, 1976; May, 1983), is possibly the most common mystical experience. Afterwards I found that it had been described by James Horne (1978) as 'casual extraverted mysticism'.

What is it like? For me now it is a simple matter of decision. I choose to be my real self. This means setting aside my ego, with all its demands for support, for feeding, for boosting, for flattering and so forth. It is obviously easier to do this in a safe atmosphere, such as a therapy session, but in more difficult situations it is sometimes worth the risk. The risk is mainly of offending or upsetting other people. Directness is so unusual in our society that it very easily seems to be untactful, even if it is well done. When in my real self, 'I don't do nice.' In therapy this seems to be all right, because it is an unusual situation where the usual expectations do not apply. I said to one client: 'I don't know why it is, but I find myself not believing a word you are saying.' He immediately owned up to being phony, and trying to avoid what he was really experiencing. With another client, I found that I thought I knew the answer to his problem, but he didn't agree. I said to him: 'I can't work with you if I think I know the answer to your problem. I think you had better find another therapist.' He agreed. It is not always about being direct. Another expression of the real self is creativity. I am continually inventing new ideas of how to work with each person in the here and now; the inventions are too numerous to mention. What it means is that the client gets the benefit of something fresh and unique, and this seems to work well.

Two quite dramatic things happened during the period when I was experiencing different kinds of groups. One was that I changed from being an introvert to being an extravert. I had always enjoyed filling in personality tests, and had felt a bit doubtful about Eysenck's statement that introversion and extraversion were biological and unchangeable. And now I know it to be false. From being an unsociable person who pre-ferred books to people, I became a sociable person who could enjoy both people and books. I could enjoy other people's company and I could enjoy my own company too.

The second dramatic thing that happened was that my atti-tude to women changed. I discovered that I had adopted a plan to get revenge on my mother, and that this had developed into a general hatred of women. In my twenties, thirties and forties I had been sexually frustrated and unsuccessful, and had been puzzled by this, because I was reasonably good-looking, had quite a manly figure and so forth, and could not imagine what was missing. All I wanted, I reasoned, was one good fuck a day – was that too much to ask? But after I had worked through my birth, and a womb experience involving killing my twin sister, I was able to abandon my hatred of women as based on an absurd misunderstanding. At the age of 50 I started on a successful sexual career which involved several women in quite good and meaningful relationships, and a few one-night stands as well. I met the woman who is now my second wife, and we became genuinely intimate. I was able to lower all my barriers and defences and be with her in quite a new way. Since we started living together 22 years ago, I have not been tempted to have sex with another woman, and this is something which I see as con-tinuing indefinitely, because it is what I want. It is my intention and my commitment; both things which I think are particularly characteristic of the Centaur stage. This relationship is a central part of my life, and very important to me. If I can have a decent relationship with one other person, with mutuality and involve-ment, this seems to me to say something about who I am and what I do.

This is of course partly because I am now one with my feel-ings as well as one with my body. The integration, the wholeness that goes with being at the Centaur stage, means that when I have an emotion I am 100 per cent behind it. I am not divided. I *am* my emotions just as I *am* my body. I learned from John Pierrakos that the body was central to everything I did. And it was from psychodrama that I particularly learned that my feelings were me, rather than something that happened to me. This is all to do with the experience of authenticity. At the Centaur stage we actually experience authenticity, as Bugental (1981) has so beautifully explained.

There was also a political side to all this. Now I am not saying that everyone who enters the Centaur stage is political, nor that when they do they are necessarily leftist. But there is something essentially critical about the Centaur stage. You cannot get to it without becoming critical of inauthenticity, which means being critical of role-playing, conventional living and what Heidegger (1962) calls 'Das Man'– which is usually translated as 'the They'. And one of the essential characteristics of authenticity is self-enactment, which is often referred to in American slang as 'walking the talk'. It is not enough to know how to talk about authenticity, it is a question of how to act authentically. As Dave Mearns (1997) has been saying in recent years, it is not enough to be trying to portray genuineness as a therapist, one actually has to *be* genuine. And this may, I only say *may*, result in some political action. Each person must find his own way, in the circumstances of his time.

I remember the excitement I felt on picking up on a second-hand bookstall the original American edition of Charles Hampden-Turner's (1971) book *Radical Man*. This was an account of what personal growth was and how it took place, and how it related to political thought and action, right within the boundaries of humanistic psychology as I understood it. What the book said was that the personal and the political are one – that personal growth leads to political radicalism. It also made it clear that authenticity in the existential sense (a combination of self-respect and self-enactment) was the major factor in any real self-development; it was the key to where one was going and also the key to getting there. The strong feeling of the real self which I had had in groups connected up with the philosophical idea of authenticity, and I felt a real connection there – that authenticity was one place where the personal and the political came together. One could not be authentic and experience alienation or anomie at the same time. This brought together the two paths (the positive path of personal growth and the negative path of radical psychology) in a way which I found very satisfying.

I don't think Maslow says enough about the political side of all this. It seems clear to me that the Centaur stage is full of political interest and implications, and this has been spelt out in many ways by people like Rollo May, Alvin Mahrer, Carl Rogers, Christian Bay, Mary Parker Follett, Walt Anderson, John Vasconcellos, Isaac Prilleltensky, Charles Hampden-Turner and others. It is a politics of enablement, of mutual empowerment, of reconciliation and conflict resolution. It is also a politics which can say 'NO' in unmistakable terms to oppression, limitation and falsification. It is just as critical of compulsions in the social order as it is of compulsions within the person, and it uses the same approach in both cases. First the task is to identify the compulsions and bring them to the surface; then the task is to work with them in such a way that they may change. This will involve both support and confrontation of the people involved. It will involve a genuine respect for what is involved, and will never believe it has the one right answer. What it does have is an enormous sense of possibility.

The difficulty with that approach to politics is that you have to find a place to stand. It has to be a place where pressure and influence can be effective. In therapy this is relatively straightforward. In organization development it is much more complex, but much can usually be done by an outside consultant who is given the necessary support, and I have done some of that work myself. In the community it is harder again to find the right place to stand – sometimes action research or participative research offers a way (Reason and Bradbury, 2000). On the national level it is very rare to be able to find the right place to stand. I am not sure about this, but perhaps Nelson Mandela found a way. However, it cost him an enormous amount; he had to invest his whole life into the project. Perhaps Gandhi might be another example, I don't really know. All I am saying is that this approach to political change works well on a small scale, but is much more difficult to operate on a large scale – and necessarily so. I have said more about this elsewhere (Rowan, 2001).

Looking back on the Centaur stage

So that was the process. It seemed to me to be a process which offered me breakthrough after breakthrough, rebirth after rebirth. As I began to consolidate all this stuff, I began to be able to be authentic at will. Instead of being something that came and went like peaks or glimpses, it became something I could choose to do.

Many people think that the implication of all this is that one becomes the real self at all times – that somehow the mental ego disappears, to be replaced by the real self. But it does not usually work like that. Certainly in my own experience of about 28 years since first contacting my real self, this is not what I have found.

The way it works for me is more like this: my mental ego – which I used to call Big Eggo – became less dominant. Instead of running things and claiming a lot of support and feeding, it became more like a commissionaire – someone who stood at the door and let visitors in or kept them out. Other subpersonalities of mine (Rowan, 1990) could have more say and more play, and my whole demeanour became more varied, more interesting and more approachable. The real self could then be called on at times when authenticity was needed and appropriate. I thought at first that the real self didn't do anything at all, but this was because I was confusing it with the causal self (Wilber, 1996). What it does is to be authentic and to walk the existential edge.

No one subpersonality, no one entity of any kind, should rule the psyche like a dictator. And this applies to the real self, too. I believe that we do not meet people who are intelligent, or neurotic, or enlightened. We only meet people who have intelligent times, who have neurotic times, who have enlightened times (Millman, 1999).

I think now that my real self has passed being a plateau experience and has become a constant adaptation. But I only become *aware* of it in case of need. At other times it is background. I believe that that is a better way of putting it. I can certainly hang on to it throughout a therapy session, and through a weekend workshop, and through a five-day workshop. I don't put it in the foreground when I read the paper, or go to Sainsbury's, or catch the train, or give a conference presentation. One of the things which has become very important to me is being a teacher as well as a therapist. Through teaching I can pass on what I have learned, both in an intellectual and in an experiential way, and through just being who I am. Through writing and through conference presentations I can pass on what seems most valuable to me.

I went through Maslow's list of characteristics of the self-actualized person, to try and see what order they came in for me. But I found to my surprise that there was no order. They all seemed to be mutually reinforcing aspects of the same thing. When I compare Maslow's descriptions of self-actualization, Rogers' account of the development of the fully functioning person, Mahrer's account of actualization and integration, May's account of the emergence of the 'I Am' feeling and Jung's account of individuation, it does seem to me as if they are all talking about the same thing: entry into the Centaur stage.

Some time ago, I got out a handout with a brief summary of Maslow's list of characteristics of the self-actualized person. Since then I have produced another handout with some more, and present it as Figure 8.2.

In the light of critiques such as that of Adorno (1986), who says that to present oneself as authentic is in itself inauthentic, I can only say that I have tried to be accurate in what I have said here. I can do no more. I must say that it feels good to be a

1. **Perception of reality** An unusual ability to detect the spurious, the fake and the dishonest in personality, and in art.
2. **Acceptance** A relative lack of overriding guilt, of crippling shame and of extreme or crippling anxiety. Lack of defensiveness.
3. **Spontaneity** Simplicity and naturalness, lack of artificiality or straining for effect. A superior awareness of their own desires, opinions and subjective reactions in general.
4. **Problem centring** Not ego-centred. They usually have some mission in life, some task to fulfil, some problem outside themselves which enlists much of their energies.
5. **Solitude** They like solitude and privacy to a definitely greater degree than the average. Self-actualizing people do not need others in the ordinary sense.
6. **Autonomy** These people can maintain a relative serenity in the midst of circumstances that would drive other people to suicide; they are self-contained.
7. **Fresh appreciation** They have the capacity to appreciate again and again, freshly and naïvely, the basic goods of life, with awe, pleasure, wonder and even ecstasy.
8. **Peak experiences** Spontaneous mystical experiences are common. Those who have them may be called peakers, and contrasted with non-peakers.
9. **Human kinship** They have a deep feeling of identification, sympathy and affection. They feel kinship and connection, as if all people were members of a single family.
10. **Humility and respect** They have a democratic character structure in the deepest sense. They are able to learn from anybody who has something to teach them.
11. **Interpersonal relationships** They can have deep and profound interpersonal relations. The other person in the relationship is often also close to self-actualization.
12. **Ethics** These individuals are strongly ethical, they have definite moral standards, they do right and do not do wrong. Needless to say, their notions of right and wrong and of good and evil are often not the conventional ones.

Figure 8.2 Characteristics of the self-actualized person.

13. **Means and ends**   They often regard as ends in themselves many experiences and activities that are, for other people, only means. They appreciate the doing itself.

14. **Humour**   They laugh at the ridiculous, but there is no hostility in their humour, and no rebellion. They don't make jokes that hurt someone else.

15. **Creativity**   They are creative in a special way; their creativity touches whatever activity they are engaged in. They even see creatively.

16. **Resistance to enculturation**   They maintain a certain detachment from the culture in which they are immersed.

17. **Imperfections**   They can be ruthless; they may be absent-minded; they may shock by lack of politeness; they may be too involved with sick people; they may have internal strife and conflicts; they can be stubborn and irritating. There are no perfect people.

18. **Values**   The topmost portion of the value system of the self-actualizing person is entirely unique. This must be true by definition, for self-actualization is actualization of a self, and no two selves are alike.

19. **Resolution of dichotomies**   The age-old opposition between head and heart, reason and instinct, thought and will disappears in healthy people; they become synergistic rather than antagonistic. Desires are in excellent accord with reason. Be healthy and then you may trust your impulses.

20. **Authenticity**   Combination of self-respect and self-enactment. 'Walks the talk.' No gap between intentions and actions. Can relate to people directly and uniquely. 'I and you' rather than 'I and it'. Coming from the centre, not from a role.

21. **Integration**   There is no split between thinking and feeling, mind and body, left brain and right brain, masculine and feminine, persona and shadow, operating potentials and deeper potentials, conscious and unconscious, and so on. If new conflicts are discovered, there is no resistance to working through them.

22. **Non-defensiveness**   More inclined to find the truth within what the other person is saying than to defend against it or try to prove it wrong. May defend own right to be different, but still not in terms of right and wrong.

continued

23. **Vision-logic**   Not constrained by the rules of formal logic. May be interested in alternative logics, such as fuzzy logic, many-valued logic or dialectical logic. 'Never let yourself be bullied by an either-or.'

24. **Paradoxical theory of change**   Beisser (1972) in the gestalt school developed a set of ideas which have been found to make a lot of sense by gestaltists. Also found in focusing, experiential psychotherapy, psychodrama, person-centred work and so on. Change occurs not by trying to go somewhere you are not, but by staying with what is. This is very different from the common idea of self-mastery.

25. **The real self**   The chart (see Figure 8.1, p. 117) shows that the idea that there is a centre and a periphery to the personality, and that the centre is true and the periphery false, is popular in the Centaur stage. The real self seems to me a crucial part of Centaur thinking, because without a real self the notion of authenticity collapses. It is a skin-encapsulated self. It is the ultimate, pure sense of 'I', considered as a separate being. That is its essence. It is quite different from the mental ego, however. It does not need all the props, the support, the boosting, the confirmation that the mental ego needs. It is a centred gyroscope with its own power supply.

26. **'I create my world'**   One of the great discoveries of the Centaur stage is that it makes sense to take responsibility to the limit, and to say that we are responsible for everything. People like Will Schutz and Alvin Mahrer have spelt this out in great detail. There are some common misunderstandings of this view, but this is not the place to go into them. (See Rowan 1998, pp. 110–12.)

27. **Intentionality**   At the Centaur stage, just because we take responsibility for our actions, we are fully behind what we do. This enables real commitment. Intentionality and commitment go very closely together.

28. **Intimacy**   Intimacy between two people is made possible only at the Centaur stage because it is only then that roles can be laid aside. You can't be intimate and be playing a role at the same time.

29. **Presence**   To be genuinely present with another person is a rare ability. Ronnie Laing could do it. Carl Rogers could do it. Again it cannot be done through role-playing. To try to portray presence is not to be present.

---

30. Openness It has been suggested (Mittelman, 1991) that openness is in fact the key element in the Centaur experience, although this has been argued against. It is certainly important in humanistic management theory.

Note: The first nineteen of these items come from Maslow (1987), abbreviated by me, the other eleven from Rowan (submitted).

---

person like this. Of all the aspects of it, I feel that the ability to be non-defensive is the most important. And this goes with the experience mentioned earlier, of now feeling superior to no one. I do think this comes very directly out of the theory and the experiences I have been describing.

Therapy and life

If I now have to say how this affects what I do as a therapist, I think that there are three main things to be said. The first is that sheer presence is very important for me. To be really present in the room with another person is the heartland of my kind of therapy. Ronnie Laing used to call it co-presence, which is perhaps an even better way of putting it. This is to say that my real self – what Virginia Satir used to call my personhood – is involved, rather than some subpersonality or role-playing. There is a lot of good stuff in the Baldwin (2000) book about this. This is a very different view from that of the psychoanalyst, or even the Jungian, because it places no emphasis at all on the unconscious. This view doesn't need to reject the unconscious, because obviously subpersonalities can be looked on as just other ways of talking about the unconscious, but there is no particular interest in the unconscious as such.

The second thing is that because I have been into so many deep places in my own therapy, confronted so many shadows, experienced so many deaths and rebirths, faced my own

why deeply phenomen

neurosis and psychosis, I feel able to go with my clients into whatever depths and frightening places they may need to go. I do not have to hold back from their prenatal material, from their Kleinian stuff, or from their big dreams and archetypal encounters. I can go with them into the darkness and into the light. I can be with them in facing what they most need and fear to face. This also applies to people I meet in everyday life. I feel as if I can meet people at all times with this underlying understanding, and this has a considerable effect on the way in which we can interact. It is as if I, as a whole person, am ready to meet the other, as a whole person. This is perhaps very close to what the existentialist writers are also saying.

The third thing is that I have the repertoire of techniques to enable my clients to do what they want to do but do not know how to do. Because I have been to so many workshops all over the world, and seen so many great therapists in action, I have at my fingertips a good range of tools to offer. As someone once said, if all you have is a cricket bat, it is creative and worthwhile to dig a hole with it, if digging a hole is what is needed now: but if you use a cricket bat when a spade is available, there is something inefficient or even inept about that. The implication of this is that presence is not enough, love is not enough, lots of own therapy is not enough, a basic approach is not enough – I as a therapist have to have enough tools at my disposal to offer the client what that client needs in order to do what they have to do. In my opinion, the tragic story of Ann France (1988) is really about three therapists, none of whom had the means to enable her to go to the depth that she needed to go to. Therapists can let people down. And one of the main ways they can let them down is by simply not knowing enough.

Some of the people who read this will know that in recent years I have also become interested in transpersonal work. This chapter simply deals with the groundwork which opened up that possibility for me. I have always liked the quotation from Eleanor Merry:

Imagine, that you are ascending a staircase which is reflected in a mirror on the floor; with every step you take in ascending the staircase you appear to take a step, in the mirror, into an abyss. With every stage of mystical communion with the elementary, planetary, and stellar powers, there was a corresponding step in knowledge of the depths of the soul and of the body. (Merry, 1962)

To me the two things are intimately connected.

So there I stand.

References

Adorno, T. W. (1986) *The Jargon of Authenticity*. Evanston: Northwestern University Press.

Anthony, D., Ecker, B. and Wilber, K. (eds) (1987) *Spiritual Choices: The Problem of Recognizing Authentic Paths to Inner Transformation*. New York: Paragon House.

Baldwin, M. (ed.) (2000) *The Use of Self in Therapy* (second edition). New York: The Haworth Press.

Beisser, A. (1972) 'The paradoxical theory of change', in J. Fagan and J. L. Shepherd (eds) *Gestalt Therapy Now*. New York: Harper.

Bugental, J. F. T. (1976) *The Search for Existential Identity*. San Francisco: Jossey-Bass.

Bugental, J. F. T. (1981) *The Search for Authenticity* (enlarged edition). New York: Irvington.

France, A. (1988) *Consuming Psychotherapy*. London: Free Association Books.

Hampden-Turner, C. (1971) *Radical Man*. London: Duckworth.

Heidegger, M. (1962) *Being and Time* (trans. John McQuarrie and Edward Robinson). New York: Harper & Row.

Horne, J. (1978) *Beyond Mysticism*. Waterloo: Wilfrid Laurier University Press.

Maslow, A. H. (1987) *Motivation and Personality* (third edition). New York: Harper & Row.

May, R. (1983) *The Discovery of Being*. New York: W. W. Norton.

Mearns, D. (1997) 'Achieving the personal development dimension in professional counsellor training', *Counselling* 8(2), 113–20.

Merry, E. (1962) *The Flaming Door: The Mission of the Celtic Folk-Soul*. Edinburgh: Floris Books.

Millman, D. (1999) Interviewed by Craig Hamilton in *What is Enlightenment?*, 15.

Mittelman, W. (1991) 'Maslow's study of self-actualisation: a reinterpretation', *Journal of Humanistic Psychology* 31(1), 14–35.

Reason, P. and Bradbury, H. (eds) (2000) *The Sage Handbook of Action Research*. London: Sage.

Rowan, J. (1989) 'A late developer', in W. Dryden and L. Spurling (eds) *On Becoming a Psychotherapist*. London: Tavistock/Routledge.

Rowan, J. (1990) *Subpersonalities*. London: Routledge.

Rowan, J. (1998) *The Reality Game* (second edition). London: Routledge.

Rowan, J. (2001) *Ordinary Ecstasy* (third edition). London: Routledge.

Rowan, J. (submitted) *The Phenomenology of the Centaur*.

Stevens, B. (1970) *Don't Push the River*. Moab: Real People Press.

Wilber, K. (1996) *The Atman Project* (second edition). Wheaton: Quest.

9 | How Do I Embody the Experiential Model of Human Beings? (Experiential Psychotherapy)

Alvin Mahrer

W HEN THE EDITORS handed me the assignment, the question they invited me to answer, one reaction I had was a kind of respectful admiration. What an honest question! How simple! What an important question, and yet it seemed that such a question was rarely asked. The next reaction I had was that I had never seriously thought about that question. When I tried to answer the question, there were some points that kept appearing before I could answer the question honestly and sincerely. Please bear with my clarifying these points before directly answering the question.

Experiential psychotherapy goes with a comprehensive model of human beings

The question I found myself addressing was this: how do I embody the experiential model of *human beings*? The question was not: how do I embody the model or theory of *experiential psychotherapy*?

For about four decades or more, I have tried to develop a psychotherapy which was finally born with the name 'experiential psychotherapy' (Mahrer, 1996). There is a conceptualization or a model that helps make some useful sense of what happens in sessions of experiential psychotherapy. But over those four decades or so, I was also steeped in trying to arrive at some position on the deeper underlying eternal issues and questions about human beings: How and why are there times when I feel so good or feel so bad? How and why did I come to be the person I seem to be? How can I understand the ways I seem to act, behave, think and feel? How and why does an infant become a person that the infant seems to become? How and why is my body the way it is? What am I like down deep inside? Down deep inside, am I similar to or different from most other people? How can I most usefully picture or think of a person, a 'personality'? How do I arrive at some way of making sense of or creating the world in which I seem to live? How and why do people seem to form groups, communities, societies? How and why can and does change seem to occur, in the way I am, in the way I act and feel and behave? How and why can larger social change occur? What kind of person can I become? What kind of world can there be? What is a helpful, useful philosophy and philosophy of science in my trying to answer these questions? What are my own answers and positions in the important questions and issues in philosophy and philosophy of science? My own attempts to answer such seemingly basic questions culminated in a comprehensive experiential model of human beings (Mahrer, 1989).

Experiential psychotherapy is the working buddy of the much more comprehensive experiential model of human beings. For me, the weaker question was how I embody the model of experiential psychotherapy, and the stronger question was how I embody the experiential model of human beings.

Embodying the experiential model came first, then the model gradually evolved

Perhaps the common picture is of some conceptualization of human beings, e.g. a psychoanalytic or social learning or biopsychological conceptualization, and then of a person who has some conceptualization to embody. This was not the way it was for me: it was more the reverse. First came my being so impressed with people who embodied rare and special changes, sometimes in experiential sessions, sometimes in wondrous other ways. By eager and careful study of those people and how they came to embody these precious changes, I was slowly able to create a helpful and hopefully useful model of human beings. The experiential model of human beings was inspired by, and always seems to lag a little behind, those rare and wondrous changes that such things as experiential sessions seemed to help bring about. Embodying the experiential model was usually a little ahead of the gradual development of the experiential model.

'Experiential persons' become more like and more unlike one another

'Experiential persons', for me, are those rare people who are able to move in the direction of becoming the optimal persons that the experiential model illuminates as possible. Embodying the experiential model seems to mean my becoming more like and more unlike these people.

In some ways, experiential persons become more like one another

The experiential model pictures a person in terms of parts that are in relation to one another. These parts are thought of as possibilities for experiencing, potentialities for experiencing, and they are pictured as relating to one another in ways that are friendly or unfriendly, loving or hateful, integrative or disintegrative. This is just about all I am, or you are: potentialities for experiencing in some kind of relationship with one another.

People whose parts are in wonderful relationship usually embody some common features

Picture what I am calling 'experiential persons' as achieving a state where more and more of their parts, their potentialities for experiencing, relate to one another in ways that are simply wonderful. The more these people achieve this state, the more they can and do embody some common features. For one thing, these people know what it is like, inside their bodies, to be in a state that can be described by words such as oneness, wholeness, unity, internal peace, harmony, tranquillity. They at least know what it is like to be in this state. They also become much more in tune with and receptive to what is going on inside, to the immediate bodily sensations, to the feeling that is happening right now, to the thoughts that are going on inside. From moment to moment, there is a heightened sensitivity and openness to their immediate inner worlds.

Another common feature of people whose parts relate so harmoniously with one another is that these people are much less inclined to build personal worlds, to construct and live in personal worlds of painful scenes, painful situations. Their personal world is built, constructed, organized, fashioned to contain and to inflict less pain, anguish, hurt, turmoil.

People who embody their deeper parts usually share some common features

People who become more and more what the experiential model says people can become have something else in common. These people seem to become more and more of what had been deeper inside. The deeper parts, the deeper potentialities for experiencing, become more and more of who and what the person is. It is as if the person that the person is undergoes continuous change, a continuous becoming, a continuous being of the deeper parts that are no longer deeper. There is a continuous process of becoming, of actualization, of evolution.

One of the common features of these people is a greater bodily-felt sense of aliveness, vitality, bodily tingling, vibrancy, excitement, buoyancy, joy. Another common feature is a heightened sense of sheer experiencing, greater depth, breadth, intensity, fullness, saturation of simple sheer experiencing. Yet another common feature is a kind of progressive shifting from being one sort of person to being a qualitatively different sort of person as each formerly deeper part tends to reconstitute who and what the changing person becomes.

The experiential model has a picture of what people can become. In some ways these people are seen as having some common features, as becoming more like one another.

In some ways, experiential persons become more unlike one another

Experiential persons are much more than just people who embody the experiential model: they are people whose whole lives are dedicated toward becoming what the experiential model says people can become. In some ways, this means that these people gradually become more unlike one another. There are some reasons for this.

One reason is that the experiential model declines the common notion that what is deeper inside most people are relatively universal basic needs, drives, motives, human characteristics, traits. Down deep inside, at our core, according to most theories, we all share a common heritage, humanness, psychobiological foundation. The experiential model has a different picture of where it all comes from in the first place, the very origins of what is deep down inside (Mahrer, 1989). Accordingly, as you and I become what you and I can become, as we become what our deeper insides offer as possibilities, you and I am likely to become more and more unlike one another. What lies deep within you may be possibilities for experiencing tenderness, gentleness, softness; a deeper potentiality for experiencing a sense of being in charge, being controlling, being dominant; a deeper potentiality for experiencing oneness, closeness, bondedness. What lies deep within me may be possibilities for experiencing violence, explosiveness, destructiveness; being risky, dangerous, adventurous; a deeper experiencing of sheer playfulness, giddiness, silliness. We will tend to become more and more unlike as each of us becomes what each of us can become.

Before you became an experiential person, you did not experience a sense of tenderness, gentleness, softness; you did not experience a sense of being in charge, controlling, dominant; you did not experience oneness, closeness, bonded-ness. These were potentialities for experiencing that lay deep inside you. As you changed, as you became the person you were capable of becoming, you became a qualitatively new person who now included these formerly deeper potentials for experiencing. Before I became an experiential person, I did not experience violence, destructiveness, explosiveness. I did not have a sense of experiencing being risky, dangerous, adventurous. I did not experience sheer playfulness, giddiness, silliness. These were deeper potentialities for experiencing that lay deep inside me. As I changed, as I became the person I was capable of becoming, I became the qualitatively new person who now included these formerly deeper potentials for experiencing. As each of us becomes the persons we are capable of becoming, as our unique deeper potentials for experiencing become the integral parts of who and what we can be, it is almost certain that we will become more and more unlike one another.

Another reason for our becoming increasingly unlike one another is that the worlds you and I build, construct, and live in will tend to become increasingly unlike. Your world will increasingly come from and provide for your own experiencings, for the experiencing of being in charge, being controlling, being dominant. My world will increasingly come from and provide for my own possibilities for experiencing, for my experiencing of playfulness, giddiness, silliness. As we become increasingly more of what we can become, our personal worlds are likely to become increasingly unlike one another.

As you and I increasingly become different persons, increasingly building and living in different worlds, then our differences can become increasingly concrete, easy to recognize, apparent. The way you walk, the place where you live, the way you move your mouth when you talk, and the people at the table when you eat, will come from and provide for your experiencings, and almost all of these things will be different in me and in my world.

When you and I both embody the experiential model, we are

likely to move in the direction of becoming what the experiential model says we can become. That usually means that there will be ways in which you and I become more and more like one another, and ways in which we become more and more unlike one another.

What are some ways that I embody the experiential model of human beings?

Writing this section is tricky because I think I know enough of the experiential model to know that I cannot get all the way out of the experiential model to get a truly clear picture of how I embody the experiential model. It is also tricky because the ways I embody the experiential model today differ from the ways I embodied the experiential model some years ago, and I would not even try to guess how I might embody the experiential model in the years to come.

How far along am I on my own journey toward becoming what I can become? It is easy to reach back and touch where I was when I started. I can also peer way ahead to what I may perhaps be able to become. I have not progressed very far.

I have experiential sessions by, for, and with myself

Every few weeks or so, I go into my office, alone, close my eyes, and spend one-and-a-half to two hours going through an experiential session (Mahrer, 1996, 2001). I begin by finding a scene of very strong feeling, usually a painful bad feeling, but sometimes a joyful good feeling. The scene of strong feeling may be in my dream world or in my daily world of today or from long ago. Scenes of powerful feeling are the precious window into my innermost deeper world.

Each session gives me a grand opportunity to become the person I am capable of becoming, to taste and sample what it is like to be the wholesale, qualitatively new person I can become. I am ready to undergo complete transformation, complete metamorphosis. This incredible shift in the very foundations of who and what I am may last only a few seconds or for ever, may make only a token or a magnificent difference in my post-session world in only a few situations or almost everywhere, for only a little while or from now on. And there is more. Each session gives me a wondrous opportunity to be free of whatever scene of painful feeling may have been front and centre for me in the beginning of this session. That painful scene is no longer here in my personal world, or it has been drained of its painful feeling.

Having regular experiential sessions is a powerful adventure to discover who and what I can become, to live and be as this whole new person, and to free my personal world of those scenes that hurt so much. These are the goals of each experiential session. I hope to have these sessions for the rest of my life.

I become whatever my insides enable me to become, rather than following some theory's version of optimal persons and optimal worlds

The experiential model has created experiential sessions that can transform me into becoming the kind of person my insides enable me to become, and to free me of the painful situations of my own personal world, and the painful feelings in those painful situations. But the experiential model has no script or predetermined agenda for the optimal person I can become or for the optimal world in which I can live.

The experiential model does not say that I should exude care and compassion, be humble and modest, be open and honest, contribute to my community, be kindly and empathic, be creative or loving or friendly or generous or nurturant. The experiential model does not have a predetermined picture of how I should be with others, how people should be with one another, what a good community should be, what an optimal world is like. The experiential model does not say that my world, or an optimal world, should be peaceful, law-abiding, kindly, free of hatred and war. There is no list of commandments or universal rights. There is no godlike voice telling about how people ought to be, what the good life is, how the world can be. There is no wise philosophy or religion to paint its picture of what the good person is like, what the good world is like. I decline all theories' versions of optimal persons and optimal worlds.

In contrast, I entrust and commit myself to becoming whatever person my experiential sessions show I can become. In addition, I entrust and commit myself to living and being in whatever world the person I become lives in, creates and builds, constructs and has. The person I become is the person that I become, and this person is the one who rides the bicycle, embraces the stranger, gives away the painting, dresses in the baggy pants, joins this organization, travels to Greece, accepts the new position, has that silly grin, lives with that person. I become what my insides allow me to become as the experiential session discovers my insides and helps them to become more and more integrated and actualized. And I build and live in the personal world that I help build and live in as I become what my insides enable me to become.

The real world is where I play; the world of experiential sessions is where I do serious work

I can think of myself as living in at least three worlds. I cherish and respect my dream world, and try to use my dreams in my experiential sessions. I also live in the world of my experiential sessions, either by myself or working with another person. These sessions are the world of serious work. And there is the real world of aeroplanes and wrenches, mothers and brothers, flowers and birds, close friends and lawyers, books and music. This is the world of joyful play, the world of actual experiencing. I do not take this world as seriously as I take my world of experiential sessions. Even my seriousness, in the real world, is laced with a hint of playfulness.

For me, the world of experiential sessions is the serious world of deep-seated change. This world holds the secrets of wondrous change. It is the serious world of exciting discovery, of incredible transformation, of unlimited possibilities. It is the world I study seriously. It is the serious world of serious change.

For me, embodying the experiential model means that I seem to think of and to live in the real world as a gigantic, irreplaceable, incredibly rich warehouse of golden opportunities for sheer experiencing, an almost unending festival of possibilities for experiencing. The real world is, for me, so far, a world of play, a world of actually undergoing what I am increasingly capable of experiencing. The experiential session shifts me into becoming a qualitatively new person. In the real world, I have opportunities to actually be, to actually undergo, to actually experience, what the serious work of the experiential session gave me a chance to be, undergo, become, experience.

Still, there are a few ways in which I do take the real world seriously. One way is that the real world, like my dream world, is a prized warehouse of scenes of strong feeling for my experiential sessions. In addition, most experiential sessions culminate with post-session homework to be carried out in the real world. That is, the experiential session is over when the session is over and I am truly being the whole new person in my real world.

For example, if I discover a deeper potential for experiencing a sense of risk, exciting danger, giddy adventurousness, then in the session I can become the qualitatively new person who literally is this whole new person. In the session, I can literally rehearse being this qualitatively new person in post-session scenes. When the session is over, as this qualitatively new person, I literally undergo this new experiencing in the rehearsed actual scenes with my neighbour, who takes me on an exciting ride on his new motorcycle, my first ride on a motorcycle, complete with daredevil howls of risky excitement. That evening, still as this qualitatively new person, there is a new-felt sense of risky adventure as Julie and I hold hands and together tip-toe into altogether new, for us, regions of culinary and erotic high adventure. The session is over when I carry out my homework as the qualitatively new person in my qualitatively new world.

With these exceptions, the real world is my play world of experiential living and being. Here is a serious way that I think I embody the experiential model.

I listen to you by having pictures and by having bodily-felt sensations

When we are together, I do not have private thoughts about you. I have no private inferences about you, no agenda of what I want from you, no private reactions to you, no hidden thoughts about how we are together, how you are with me or how I am with you. I do not plan what I will say or do with you. I do not analyse what you say and do, flag something for later study, try to find some deeper meaning in what you say and do or do not say and do. I do not try to be some way with you, try to impress you in some way, try to get you to think of me as like this or like that. I do not try to know what you are really like, to make sense of you, to identify what kind or type of person you are, to probe inside you, to categorize you. I do not try to play some role with you, to be your best friend, your companion, your lover, your parent, your child, your follower, your admirer, your buddy, your confidante, your sparring partner, your hero, your seducer, your victim.

When I am with you, I try to be fully attuned to the pictures that come to me when I listen attentively to what you say, and when I pay careful attention to what you do. I get pictures when I am with you. I try to be sensitive to the flow of these pictures. I try to be exceedingly honest in allowing these pictures to occur, and in seeing what these pictures are. When I am truly with you, I have pictures that you set off in me. I trust these pictures. They are the meaning you bring forth in me.

When you say words, I do my best to position myself so that what you say and how you say what you say can bring forth pictures in me. Positioning myself means that I try to listen carefully to what you say, almost as if your words, and how you say what you say, are somehow also coming in and from and through me too.

When I listen carefully, I get pictures. Sometimes the pictures are cloudy, hazy, unclear. Then I may invite you, if you wish, to help make the picture clearer, closer to what you may have in mind. Usually the pictures are rather specific and explicit. Then I may invite you, if you are willing, to correct what I picture, to make my picture more accurate in terms of what you do mean. Sometimes I know that my pictures come more from me than from what you are saying, from what you mean and have in mind. In any case, listening to you is largely my getting pictures, and being with you is partly being able to share, to tell about, to offer the pictures I have as I am being with you.

When I am with you, I get bodily-felt sensations. Sometimes the pictures come from the bodily-felt sensations. Sometimes the bodily-felt sensations come from the pictures. The pictures and the bodily-felt sensations go together in me. Sometimes the bodily-felt sensations are subtle and light, or pounding and compelling. Sometimes they are pleasant and joyful, or painful, ominous, rumbling, unpleasant. I try to cultivate and to have these pictures and these bodily sensations. I try to rely on them, and only on them. They constitute what you are when I am with you. I try to have, to know, and to trust these pictures and these bodily-felt sensations.

When you say 'My daughter is coming home', and when you seem to say these words in that particular way, I mainly see the pictures I see and I have the bodily sensations I have. I see you at the front door, flinging it open, and here is your daughter, the two of you beaming at one another, and I have bodily sensations of tingly lightness in my chest.

How I am with you can come in part from my pictures and bodily-felt sensations. I can simply offer these pictures and bodily sensations to you. When I listen carefully to you, here is the simple, honest, candid picture I have and, if you want, here are the accompanying bodily-felt sensations. Or I can invite you to fill in, clarify, correct what is probably incomplete, missing, vague, wrong in my picture. 'My daughter is coming home.' I have a cloudy, wispy, fragmented picture of her as having been far away for a long time, and as coming home soon. No, I am wrong on all counts. Oh, now my picture is more filled in, more accurate. Sometimes my pictures become more filled in, accurate, concrete. Sometimes there are all sorts of exciting new pictures, with new bodily-felt accompanying sensations. How I am with you can come from the pictures and bodily-felt sensations that seem so easily brought about when I pay close and honest attention to what you are doing and saying.

On special rare occasions, we can both be attending to something of real meaning and importance to you, rather than attending mainly to one another. When we are both attending fully to that photograph of you as a child, or to your memory of playing the violin many years ago, or to the cancer in your lung, then the pictures and bodily sensations I have just might resonate from something much deeper in you, perhaps. You may have allowed me to get pictures of something very deep about you and your daughter, about you as a photographed child, about the memory of you playing the violin, about that cancer in your lung.

But, accurate or not, coming mainly from you or mainly from me, I often listen to what you do and say by relying a great deal on the pictures I get and the bodily-felt sensations I have. This is not all I am when I am with you. But when I listen carefully and attentively to you, much of how I am comes from the rich flow of pictures and bodily-felt sensations.

Each moment is an adventure of becoming and being the person I am capable of becoming and being

If I am successful, if I am the way I yearn to be, I will be the fullest possible me in this moment, I will be the person I am capable of being. If I embody what the experiential model offers, its highest value, there are two ways that each moment can be an adventure of becoming and being the person I am capable of becoming and being.

One is that I will be experiencing what I am capable of

experiencing. The experiencing is full rather than partial, saturated rather than muted, alive rather than dead, deeper rather than superficial, direct rather than indirect, honest rather than dishonest, open rather than closed, coming from the person I am capable of becoming rather than coming from the ordinary continuing person who draws back away from the person I am capable of becoming.

Second, the balance of what I am welcomes and loves the experiencing that I am right now. There is a sense of oneness, of being a whole person, of each part lovingly smiling at all other parts. It is a sense of internal harmony, togetherness, peacefulness, tranquillity. All parts of me are friendly to the experiencing that I am right now. This is called integration.

If I am truly successful, I enter into this moment in the real world with a sense of pleasantly risked adventure. Can I be fully me in this unfolding moment? What kind of wonderful experiencing can occur in this moment I am entering into? There is a sense of looking forward to, of adventure, an excitingly playful anticipation of the ready experiencing. If I am truly successful, then I am filled with a continuing sense of light, joy, giddiness, playfulness, and enjoyment in the way I am in my real world. If I am truly successful, and this is a big if, then embodying the experiential model means approaching and entering into each unfolding moment of the real world as a magnificent opportunity to be the fullest and best possible me that I can be.

I treasure other parts of me being able to say what they have to say

When I am some way, when I say or do this or that, there are usually other parts of me that have their own personal reactions. These other parts may be pleased, proud, approving, or they may be offended, critical, disgusted. Embodying the experiential model means that I can give voice to their personal reactions: 'I did a pretty good job! . . . I don't have the least idea what I am trying to say! . . . Wasn't that considerate? I am so considerate . . . What I just did was kind of dumb, right? . . . Look at the way I eat! I eat like a pig!'

I treasure being able to give voice to parts that differ wholesomely with one another: 'Do I want to enter into this almost contractual understanding with you? . . . Yes, it sounds exciting! I sure do! What a great idea! . . . No way! I hate getting caught in serious commitments! That's scary!' I treasure acknowledging the play of voices in me, especially if they are unfitting, inappropriate, raucous, impulsive, problematic, troublemaking, or if they are uncharacteristically sweet, thoughtful, innocent, naïve, touching, precious, tender. I treasure a ready willingness to try on the parts of me that you see, discern, attribute, offer, invite. 'I am cheap? OK, let's see. "Then you leave the tip. I am too damned cheap." My God, you are right! It fits! Yes it does!'

I treasure replacing the executive, removed, watchful, observing self with the trusted flow of inner experiencing, especially as guided by bodily-felt sensations

When I am in the state I want to be in, when I am the way I value being, then that sense of removed executive awareness, watchfulness, that sense of a conscious observing 'I-ness' recedes. Or perhaps it is replaced with a kind of dim glow of approving playfulness, a friendly sense of the lightly ridiculous. Whatever it is, there is a pleasant sense of entrusting myself to the simple flow of inner experiencing so that I become the immediate experiencing that is here right now. I have achieved the being of the inner experiencings that I can be. Furthermore, the flow of inner experiencings is guided by the immediate bodily-felt sensations. When these bodily-felt sensations are good and pleasant, the inner experiencing flourishes, carries forward, opens the way to the next inner experiencing. When the bodily-felt sensations are painful and bad, then something is probably wrong, experiencing stops, the danger signs are up.

I pay a price for trying to be the fullest possible me in this moment in the real world

To the extent that I have succeeded, even a little bit, in coming closer to my own inner experiencings, to the bodily-felt feelings in me, I often pay a hefty price. These inner experiencings and bodily-felt feelings are by no means always pleasant sources of joy. They can be painful, troubling, hurtful. There are times, lots of times, when my honed receptivity to what is inside makes me so vulnerable to painful, troubling, hurtful inner stirrings, rumblings, reactions, glows, percolations, flashes. This is one side of a price to pay. There is another side.

Because I am becoming more open to my insides, I am now more vulnerable to inner parts of me that are not happy with how I just was, that scold me, berate me, judge me, yell at me, are disgusted with me, are disappointed in me, hate me, make me feel just awful: 'What a terrible thing you just did . . . What you just said was a lie . . . How could you be like this? . . . Do it again, idiot, and try to do it right this time . . . You are miserable . . . Do you have any idea what you just did? . . . What the hell are you doing? . . . Are you listening to what you are saying? . . . Oh no! You screwed up again . . . Nice try. You are at least consistent, consistently awful . . .'

I am utterly terrified of a state of being closed off from myself, from my inner experiencings, of being a mechanical automaton

I am terrified of waking up, some minutes from now, or some days or years from now, and realizing with horror that I have been asleep, in a coma, dead, sleepwalking through my life. I have an even more terrifying dread of never waking up!

In this state, I am closed off from the inner experiencings in me, not touching or touched by them, cut off from my own insides. In this state, I am also closed off from what is outside me, a world that I create and in which I suffer as a continuing dead person who is numb to experiencings in the world. Sometimes, in this state, there is no sense of I-ness, of being me. I am merely dead respondings and reactings, mechanical actings and behavings. Sometimes, in this state, there is a false and illusory sense of I-ness. Sometimes, in this state, there is an exceedingly vigilant sense of I-ness, of self, and I exist in being removed, watchful, sizing things up, planning next moves, directing things from a safe position well back of danger, of true experiencings.

In this super-vigilant state, I am watchful and aware of you out there. I am conscious and aware of me over here. I can even be conscious and aware of the 'I' that is conscious and aware. I have a stream of private thoughts, ideas, inferences, and these too are kept private, removed, hidden, unless I choose to reveal little bits and pieces of what they are. There is a safely removed, unreachable, inviolate sense of self that I protect, nurture, keep safe, watch out for, preserve from ever-present danger and threat. I live inside my shell, underneath my carapace, my fortress so well protected by a moat. And yet I am so vulnerable, so exposed, so in danger. The danger is from outside, from you, and from inside, from my own cut-off, sealed-off, deeper experiencings.

I am so terrified of succumbing, or having already succumbed, to a state of believing that I am a person, that I am me, that I am a full version of who and what I can be, and never finding out that I have been dead, a virtual person, a tricked person, a less-than-I-can-be tiny person, an ordinary, normal, mechanical automaton who is truly asleep, dead, without knowing that I am asleep, dead. This is my dreadful terror.

How do I embody the experiential model in my professional life?

It seems hard to free myself of the experiential model in order to answer this question. People who know me rather well could probably give better answers than I can. Yet it certainly seems that who I am and what I do in my professional life ought to embody the experiential model because the same person sculpted out the model and lives the professional life.

As a teacher, I try to help you go deeper inside to discover your own personal framework

Picture a group of students in a class. Picture a group of trainees who are learning about psychotherapy. In both settings, my intent is to show you how to go deeper inside yourself, into your own notions and ideas, and to discover your own personal way of thinking, your own deeper notions and ideas, your own personal position on basic issues and your own personal answer to fundamental questions. I believe that I embody the experiential model by enabling you to become the student and trainee that you are capable of becoming.

You may discover that your own personal framework is psychoanalytic or Jungian or Skinnerian or cognitive or like some other established system. Or it may turn out to be your own distinctive personal framework. Whatever it may be, my job is to help you discover and develop your own personal framework into whatever it can become. I do not try to get you to know and adopt my experiential model of human beings or my experiential psychotherapy. I do that only with the tiny proportion of students and trainees whose own deeper personal framework seems to fit hand-in-glove with my own, if they are so inclined.

As a researcher, I try to discover the secrets of what psychotherapy can do, and how to do it better and better

When the experiential model fashions its own picture of research, I am led to an adventure of discovering what psychotherapy can do, can help bring about, and to discovering better and better ways of accomplishing what psychotherapy can accomplish. Embodying the experiential model means doing this kind of research for this reason. It also means helping to give birth to a discovery-oriented way of thinking about and doing research. And it means using research to help psychotherapy become more and more of what it is capable of becoming.

As a practitioner-teacher, I try to show you how to have your own experiential sessions

Picture a person who is going through an experiential session by herself. Picture a person who is going through an experiential session with me as the practitioner-teacher. In both pictures, my aim is for the person to be able to have their own experiential sessions if they are so inclined.

Whether the session is by yourself or with me, each session has the goal of enabling you to discover what is deeper inside you, of enabling you to become more and more of the person you are capable of becoming, and of enabling you to be free of the painful scene, and the painful feeling in the scene, that was front and centre for you in the session. Embodying the experiential model means that I show you how to have your own experiential sessions, if you wish. You can become your own practitioner. My teaching can consist of direct teaching, coaching, guiding, and this may or may not include my having sessions with you, sessions aimed at developing your own skills toward having your own experiential sessions, if you wish.

As a philosopher of science, I can play with the whole field of psychotherapy

When I look at the field of psychotherapy through philosophy of science, the whole field goes topsy-turvy. Everything is different. I see what I could never see before. I feel, and the field looks, amazing, ridiculous, fascinating, altogether new, utterly playful, hilarious, childlike, crazifying, out of the bounds of reality, whimsical, funny, silly. I treasure philosophy of science for allowing me to see the field this way.

I also treasure the feeling and the opportunity to try to revolutionize the whole field, from its theories to its practices, from its research to its education-training; to be seriously respectful of what the field could become, and aggressively disrespectful of what the field is; to be able to punch and poke the field, and to consider the field as a loyal buddy; to see all the glaring holes, impossible problems, wrong and eroded foundations, misbegotten pomposity, frivolous pseudoscientificality, and for me to flip back and forth between dismissing the field to the destiny it deserves and doing my best to help fix the field so that it can become what it is capable of becoming. Thank you, philosophy of science, for allowing me to have these special personal feelings.

As a human being, I try to find my own way to enable the whole world to become what it can become

The experiential model says that I can achieve magnificent changes in the personal world in which I am. The experiential model says that you and I can achieve magnificent changes in our world when you and I each become more and more of the person you can become and I can become.

My way of engaging in widespread social change, in the bettering of the larger and larger worlds which we collectively fashion, build, construct, and live in is exceedingly unrealistic, virtually impossible, laughably impractical. It is also clearly grandiose and arrogantly pompous. Furthermore, it is incredibly passive, hands-off, grindingly slow, maddeningly individualistic. I simply invite you and you and you to have experiential sessions, if you are so inclined, from now on, for the rest of your lives. If we can collectively become the persons we are capable of becoming, then, over centuries and centuries, we are taking baby steps toward enabling our whole world to become what it is capable of becoming.

Conclusions and invitations

1. There seem to be some ways that I do tend to embody my experiential model of human beings and of psychotherapy.
2. If these ways of embodying the experiential model are appealing to you, then I invite you to become familiar with this model, to consider making it your own, and to help make it better.
3. I invite you to allow the way you are to help determine the

theory or model you espouse, and also to allow whatever theory or model you espouse to help you embody that theory or model in the ways you actually are. If you are not embodying your theory or model, then it seems to me that perhaps (a) you have some work to do in order to embody your own theory or model, or (b) the theory or model you have may well be replaced by one that you can more fittingly embody.

References

Mahrer, A. R. (1989) *Experiencing: A Humanistic Theory of Psychology and Psychiatry*. Ottawa: University of Ottawa Press.

Mahrer, A. R. (1996) *The Complete Guide to Experiential Psychotherapy*. New York: John Wiley and Sons.

Mahrer, A. R. (2001) *To Become the Person You Can Become: The Complete Guide to Self-Transformation*. Palo Alto, California: Bull Publishing.

10 Embodied Theories: A Preliminary Analysis

Ernesto Spinelli and Sue Marshall

A S EDITORS of this collection of highly individual and thought-provoking chapters, we have been impressed and delighted by the honesty and openness with which all the authors have addressed the questions we put to them. It takes a certain kind of courage to expose yourself in the way that we were inviting our contributors to do. Many of them have written at length elsewhere on the subject of the theories behind their model, or even their own personal journey as psychotherapists. But this was a different project – and one which we hoped would produce something unique and intensely personal about how the models in question affect and impact upon the lives and experiences of the individual practitioners.

In this final chapter we want to attempt an overview of the accounts provided by our authors. This is not intended to be a comparison of the different chapters with any kind of measure of our own as to which authors 'best' embody their models, or which accounts seem most self-revealing, or anything of that kind. We had no preconceptions, no underlying assumptions about how a therapist *should* be a living embodiment of the model he or she chooses to practise. The impetus behind this project was one of a descriptively focused curiosity open to whatever would emerge.

In some instances we invited our contributors to amend or expand parts of their draft documents. Such suggestions were intended to permit a further highlighting and clarification of the author's statements, usually through concrete examples. The purpose was to provide the reader with specific 'lived' illustrations of the way the model plays a part in the experience of the practitioner. At no point did we attempt to criticize or place doubt upon the contributor's viewpoint.

It follows from this that each account is by definition equally valid. There is no secret blue-print by which we evaluated the chapters. We were struck both by the diversity of the accounts and by the, sometimes surprising, resonances between them. Each chapter offers unique insights into the chosen ways of being – life experiences, thoughts and feelings – of its author. As such, each chapter carries equal value and weight, and each in its own way gives rise to further questions, provokes different ideas and points towards new areas of discourse.

Similarly there was no intention to use these accounts as a way of attempting to formulate any kind of overall or generalized answer to the question 'How do psychotherapists embody their theories?' We are not trying to evolve some kind of meta-theory along such or any other lines. In our overview of the accounts we intend to stay with what the authors have said, to remain as true as possible to the individual flavour and emphasis of each narrative, rather than attempt to make deductions or assumptions about what is 'hidden' or could be inferred.

We want to look at what has been said in each narrative, and also at what has not been said. Some of the questions which emerge for us are:

- How have the individual authors approached the project?
- What is the overall emphasis of each chapter?
- What is the nature of each narrative, and what does that tell us, if anything, about the model in question, or the practitioner?
- How do the chapters vary in structure and approach?
- Are there any overall themes or ideas which emerge in the book as a whole?

- In what ways and to what extent do the individual accounts differ?
- Are there any striking similarities or convergences among them?

We were clearly interested in the way our authors related to their chosen model, in their work and also in their social and personal lives. Of equal interest was the related question of how they initially 'chose' their model; or indeed whether they even viewed it in those terms. Having 'found', 'chosen' or 'evolved' the model, what impact did it have upon them? Did this process constitute a confirmation of previously held views, or did it effect the beginning of a new way of looking at things, people, oneself? In addressing these questions we are not attempting to evoke definitive answers or truths but to highlight what may be new questions, new ideas, perhaps also uncertainties and imponderables we cannot explain or understand. We are hopeful also that the discussion arising from these chapters will provide the impetus for further areas of analysis or discourse.

Our contributors were given a number of questions to address, as described in the introductory chapter. Not all the authors chose to engage with all the questions. The areas which all the authors addressed most comprehensively were those relating to their work as psychotherapists. In some respects this is not at all surprising – one would expect eminent practitioners to be articulate about their professional lives in this kind of way. Over and above this, there is a willingness to engage with the issue of how, if at all, the theories they espouse have challenged their ideas or changed the way they view themselves, their work and their relationships outside work. In all cases there was remarkable clarity about the issue of how they had 'chosen' their model of psychotherapy.

Several authors highlighted what they saw to be the issue of the necessity or desirability of a psychotherapist embodying his or her theories. Without this, they argued, a practitioner can have no integrity. This is expressed particularly well by Anthony

Stevens in his opening remarks. All the chapters contain to some extent an account of the impact the theories espoused by the individual have had on their lives outside the orbit of their professional activities, their personal relationships and social interactions. The extent to which this is addressed varies quite considerably. In some instances the author is quite explicit about the fact that, as a whole, the theories of the model have no relevance to certain areas of his or her life. Windy Dryden is admirably clear in this respect. In other instances the author sees the theories underlying the model as representing something akin to a philosophy of living; by definition they infuse all areas of experience. This appears to be particularly so for Alvin Mahrer and Malcolm Parlett.

Two areas of discourse stand out as having been picked up by only a few of our contributors. The first is the question as to which aspects of the theory or theories they espouse have little or no impact on the person's life as currently lived and experienced. In other words, we were asking, are there any bits of the theory which do not seem to fit your experience of living? Only two authors chose to specifically address this question, although in other accounts the answer is implicit. The second question which remained largely unanswered is the hypothetical one which asked the authors what they thought they would be like now if they had not come across their theoretical model. For us the issue is raised as to whether these were worthwhile questions. That they were not is indeed a possibility, though we feel that the answers we did receive are sufficiently insightful and revealing to justify our having posed these questions in the first instance. One author was specific in the correspondence about choosing not to address the second question. It would appear that for some authors these questions were not viewed as being fruitful as a way of explaining and clarifying the way they feel they embody their model. Our sense is that, in a general way, the authors focused on, or wrote at most length about, those questions which provided for them the means of best exploring their particular relationship with their model.

The accounts provided by the different authors vary enormously in their structure, overall emphasis and the nature of the narrative itself. In some cases there is a clear structured format laid out at the beginning of the chapter. In other chapters there is almost a chronological framework; or alternatively the chapter is organized round the impact the writer's model has on different areas of his or her life. In some the feeling is that the writer specifically chooses not to have a formal predetermined structure, but waits to see what emerges in the process of the writing. This latter is the case with both Malcolm Parlett and Miles Groth, and appears to be closely related to their respective models. Indeed, Miles Groth cites this approach to writing as an example of his recognition that 'insight is a form of existential change'. Is it the case also, we wonder, that the chapters that are very structured reflect in a similar way something about the nature of the model? Perhaps so, in that the models as understood by their authors do appear to provide a perspective on life and the way it is approached which to some extent is reflected in the way each author engages with the subject matter.

There is huge variation also in the weight given to the evolution of the theory behind the model, and the relative emphasis on 'then' and 'now'. Clearly some models are 'younger' than others and perhaps one would expect those models which are more rooted in the past, in the historical sense of when they were first formulated, to give rise to an account with greater reference to the founding fathers of psychotherapy. In fact, this is not always the case. Similarly, models differ very significantly in the emphasis they place on the part played by past events and experiences in our understanding of ourselves in the present. The models represented in this book cover a wide spectrum, from those that give considerable weight to past events and their causality, to those that focus primarily on our understanding of our present experience. The reader may be surprised to find that in some cases where you might expect a predominantly now-focused account, the author writes more about *what was* as a way of describing the impact of the model on his or her life. Similarly, where you would be justified in expecting a causal narrative, this expectation is not always met. This can perhaps be seen in the chapters on psychodynamic psychotherapy and humanistic–integrative psychotherapy. The reader might expect a narrative with greater reference to past events and their impact on the present in the former than the latter; in fact the opposite is the case. There appear to be implications here about the relationship between the individual and the theory. It is not always as close as might be expected, and one's personal experience of oneself may be articulated in terms that do not necessarily emerge directly from the model espoused.

There is great variety too in the space given to elucidation, clarification and application of key concepts within the various models. Some authors are quite specific about this, focusing in detail on those concepts which appear to play a significant part in their experience of living. Others approach this whole topic in a more general way, reflecting philosophically on their life and work as a whole, rather than citing specific concepts or theories as a way of illustrating their narrative. In some cases the writers highlight the constantly changing and evolving nature of their model, their understanding and application of the model, and, indeed, of themselves as individuals, reflecting that what they write now is necessarily different from what they would have written in the past, or what they might say in the future (for example Alvin Mahrer and Malcolm Parlett). With other accounts, perhaps those of Dorothy Rowe and Windy Dryden in particular, there is a greater feeling that the authors have arrived at an understanding of their model, and their relationship to it, with which they are comfortable and which is unlikely to change greatly in the future.

The notion of change is a central concept in the enterprise of psychotherapy. To what extent do we or can we change in the course of our lives? Assuming that change is possible to some degree, what are the factors that effect change? To what extent do we have control over any changes we experience in ourselves? How fundamental or long-lasting are these changes? And what stance does psychotherapy take on this? Is the purpose of therapy to facilitate change in clients? This is an ongoing and extensive debate. One would expect a model of psychotherapy to have a view on the notion of change, and indeed it is a recurring theme in all the chapters in the book.

As we were inviting our authors to focus primarily on themselves, what emerges is a collection of highly individual accounts of the way in which each one views his or her own development, as an individual and as a practitioner. The extent to which each writer appears to feel that he or she has changed, and the degree to which each views further changes as possible or desirable seem to be crucial and central elements both of each individual's view of himself or herself, and of the relationship with the model to which he or she adheres. Some authors describe the way they encountered the model they now practise as facilitating changes in themselves which were quite dramatic, and experienced as intense, even painful and difficult at times. John Rowan's account is a good example of this, describing vividly how he learnt to identify and embrace what he calls a 'complete set of feelings' and the change encompassed in his movement to seeing himself as an extravert rather than an introvert. Michael Jacobs also gives us an account of the changes he has observed in himself over the years; he is aware that he is not the same person he was before he came across his model. However, he sets this in the context of a discussion about the extent to which those changes are the result of the theories behind his model, and the extent to which they are due to other, completely extraneous influences. This is a question raised by others too: would those changes have happened anyway? Is it perhaps that our chosen model provides us with a language or framework in which to articulate or view the course of our personal history rather than the theories themselves constituting the principal elements which provoke change?

The answer to this appears to be both 'Yes' and 'No'. Many

of the accounts provide evidence that indeed it was a specific piece of theory, or application of a concept that was the catalyst, setting off a change that was experienced, in some instances, as transformational. In other instances the change was more minor, but nonetheless significant. On the other hand, it can be observed that *all* the authors appear to experience a high degree of comfort with the language that their model provides for them. It is as though the model has facilitated their articulation of their understanding of who they are; it has given them a voice with which to express this in a way that is personally meaningful. This appears to be so even when the author is not reporting a high degree of change within himself or herself as a result of the encounter with the model.

This latter position is the one expressed by Dorothy Rowe, who takes the view that our ideas and personality are formed by early experiences and change little throughout our lives. We may develop over the years, or modify our views somewhat, but the central notions by which we conduct ourselves remain constant. An extension or modification of this view is provided by other authors in the idea that the changes we experience in the course of our lives are fundamentally a process of our discovering who we essentially are. We may make choices (perhaps helped by the concepts or techniques encountered in a psychotherapeutic model) which enable us to refine the persons we are, perhaps by enhancing those characteristics we admire in ourselves, or by reducing or minimizing those elements with which we are less comfortable, but our development as individuals is more one of discovering what is already there, rather than changing that in any fundamental way, or indeed becoming something we were not at the outset.

Yet other accounts view change as a notion with far-reaching possibilities. The idea of self-development, within oneself and one's clients, is central to the philosophy underlying the model. It is an ongoing and continuous process; in some cases, for example Mahrer's experiential psychotherapy, this process is in effect the central thrust of the model. An experiential session is *intended* to bring about change. The focus is on becoming more 'who you are', in the sense of the parts of you that had been hidden, undeveloped, unrealized. But there is an over-riding sense of those untapped potentialities being more or less limitless.

Another theme which emerges in many of the accounts is the idea of being an individualist, a free-thinker, the notion of striking out for oneself, going it alone. Perhaps this is an inevitable response to being invited to write about a subject which presupposes adherence to a particular body of thought, with the assumption of belonging to a particular group of people with similar ideas and practices. Many people, psychotherapists or not, experience the tension between the attractions of membership of a 'club' and the disinclination to be identified only or even partly by that membership or be seen as representative of what that club stands for. Some of the authors in this collection are at pains to stress that their particular model is not dogmatic or rigid, but encourages its practitioners to be individualistic and creative, presumably within certain parameters. Yet others emphasize the fact that within their model they have carved out an individual stance. This may have involved discounting or setting to one side elements of theory, or interpretations of the model which they could not wholly accept. Achieving this is not portrayed as problematic. The important thing here seems to have been to arrive at an individual understanding of, and relationship with, the model which felt appropriate for the person concerned. In several accounts it is stressed that the writer speaks for himself or herself alone, rather than as a representative of a particular model or orientation. In reflecting on this theme, we wondered if perhaps it is a function more of the people we invited to participate in the book, all of whom have attained a certain standing and level of achievement within their profession, rather than necessarily being a reflection of the theories underpinning the different models. Perhaps the ability to be somewhat different, to challenge accepted practices and ways of thought, is something which is arrived at with experience. Or perhaps having that quality or characteristic in itself contributes to a person's rising to eminence within his or her field.

It is not surprising that the notion of embodying the psychotherapeutic model should give rise to reflections on the relationship between the mind, or psyche and the body. Like the concept of change, the emphasis placed on this relationship varies enormously across the spectrum of different models and approaches. Much as one would expect, those practitioners who espouse theories relating more to cognitive processes say less about the body than authors whose models specifically encompass attention to physical sensations as part of the overall view of human functioning. Several authors state the view that the mind and the body are closely related, or even inseparable. What impinges on one inevitably affects the other. It follows from this that in order to understand ourselves, and also to take care of ourselves holistically, we need to pay attention to our bodies as an intrinsic part of our being. We are given examples of this in several accounts: in Mahrer's attention to 'bodily-felt sensations', in Rowan's account of integration and the kind of personal relationship that resulted from that for him; and in Stevens' description of his unique daily routine arising from his observance of his natural rhythms. The part played by the body in the account written by Miles Groth is of a rather different nature. His distinction between 'the body I am' and 'the body I have', and the ensuing discussion, appear to encapsulate what for him are many of the key concepts of existential psychotherapy. The title of his chapter attests to the centrality he gives to this aspect of his experience of his model.

Discussion of the therapeutic practice and application of the theories underlying the models appears in all the chapters. However, this subject is approached in a variety of different ways. Some authors have provided very clear and detailed examples of dialogues with clients to illustrate ways in which particular concepts are applied. There are different techniques which are specific to different models. In such cases the authors invariably also indicate how and to what effect they have applied these techniques in their own lives. In other accounts the psychotherapeutic focus is more on the philosophical indications of the model at the level of relating to the client, and, outside the consulting room, relating to the other person, be it friend, colleague or partner. It is interesting to note, however, that in some accounts where the focus is primarily philosophical and the model itself is not heavily technique-laden, the practitioner describes the application of theories in his or her own life in a way which is relatively action-oriented. This is apparent in the accounts of both Alvin Mahrer and Malcolm Parlett, where we are given some fascinating insights into the practical application of models whose philosophical implications clearly infuse all areas of these practitioners' lives.

When we approached the issue of how our various authors 'chose', 'came across', or 'found' their different models we were struck by the fact that, in general terms, they seemed to divide into two distinct groups: those for whom the model confirmed previously held ideas, and those for whom such earlier concepts were altered, expanded on or even demolished by the model in question. As editors, both of our experiences had been, broadly speaking, in the latter category, and one of the many repercussions of our involvement in this project has perhaps been to challenge an assumption, which may not have been explicitly formulated as such, that this was an experience common to all psychotherapists.

As mentioned at the beginning of this chapter, all our authors appeared to have no difficulty in addressing this question. Whichever camp they fell into, their encounter with their model seems to be a central part of their relationship with it. It is fascinating that three authors (Windy Dryden, Malcolm Parlett and Anthony Stevens) use almost exactly the same words in describing the experience of discovering or encountering their model – they say it was like coming home. This expression seems to indicate a significant level of comfort, of affirmation or discovering something which resonates with one's being at a deep level.

On closer examination, however, it is not as simple as a clear division into two groups. Even those authors who tell us that the model seemed to 'fit' who they were, are aware, to varying degrees, of the changes that were effected by their encounter with this particular body of theory. There are also other factors at play. Who we are at the time we encounter a new idea, concept or theory will play a part in how we respond to it, as well as the nature of that idea or concept. Thus, if a person's encounter with a model had the effect of opening up new vistas, facilitating a new and different way of experiencing life, maybe that too can be viewed as a 'fit' in that the individual concerned had, at some level, to be ready for that experience in order for it to happen. This circular interplay between who we are, what we encounter and the environment in which the encounter occurs is eloquently described by Michael Jacobs in the opening paragraphs of his chapter.

What we seem to have, therefore, is more akin to a spectrum of response to the model when first encountered, varying from a sense of it almost totally affirming and confirming previously held views and ideas, to the experience leading to a qualitatively different understanding of oneself and others. Within that spectrum there are different degrees to which each author tends more toward one end or the other. Some authors were closely involved in the establishment of their model in the first instance; many are engaged in its evolution and continuing development. All contribute, or have contributed, to their model's application, interpretation and dissemination, by becoming involved in the professional bodies and associations relevant to their model; by teaching and setting up training courses; by engaging in research and writing books and papers. As such they have severally played a significant part in shaping the course which their model has taken and is taking. In addition, therefore, to their models having an impact on them as individuals, they in their turn have an impact on their models.

As we have seen, there are both similarities and differences in the accounts contained in this book. Some ideas and themes appear repeatedly in the different chapters, others are picked up by some and not by others. Each chapter has its own distinct flavour and emphasis. Every author, however, in his or her own unique way, fully engages in an encounter with himself or herself. What emerges from that, we feel, is something which resonates across all the accounts and which is similar to the reports we frequently hear from our clients; namely that it is that encounter – between two people or with yourself – which is the crucial experience rather than an understanding of any piece of theory. In all the narratives provided by our contributors, the pivotal ideas, whatever theories underpinned them, seem to focus on the experience of relating to oneself. The individual models appear to provide a framework, with a range of different characteristics and emphases, within which this encounter takes place.

Does this, we wonder, take us any way in attempting to address one of the issues raised in the introductory overview – namely the ongoing debate about what makes psychotherapy work? What are the elements of the encounter between therapist and client that contribute to that experience being (generally speaking) of benefit? What seems to emerge from these chapters is that one significant element is the extent to which the model, and also the terms in which it is expressed, resonates with the individual concerned. Several of our authors reported unproductive encounters with other models before lighting upon the one that 'spoke' to them. It would seem that there has to be sufficient 'fit' between model and individual for the relationship between the two to be experienced as fruitful and for that to lead to the model informing the lived experience of the person concerned. The fit does not have to be perfect – indeed these chapters demonstrate again and again that some degree of disagreement or dissonance can in itself be creative and growth-inducing. But there has to be a response to the model that contains a recognition of its meaning on a 'felt' rather than an intellectual level. And this 'felt' recognition or response has to be vivid and maybe even startling in its impact.

The effect that this produces is, as mentioned above, an encounter with oneself which is illuminating, affirming and contains the potential for change and growth. It would seem to follow from this that in order for clients to experience such an encounter they need to engage with a model that is the right one for them, at the right moment, and as practised by a therapist with whom they are able to relate meaningfully on a personal level. Furthermore, it could be suggested that without the therapist himself or herself embodying the model to a significant extent, the chances of the therapeutic relationship being of benefit to the client are considerably diminished.

The notion of embodiment, therefore, seems to be understood and experienced in a variety of different ways. The differences are sometimes as one would expect from the model that the individual practises. In other cases this is not so. What emerges, for us, throughout all of the chapters, is that it is the inter-relationship between the individual author and his or her model that permits that lived sense of embodiment – in whole or part – expressed by our contributors. Furthermore, this embodiment is not solely directed toward the individual person but also, and significantly, toward the theory itself. It appears to us that it is this living, interactive quality infusing all of the chapters which provides them with not only their uniqueness but also their point of convergence with each other. Perhaps, as readers may have discerned for themselves, it is a convergence that extends to all examples of embodied theories.